Anarchist [KU-602-633]

VOLUME 15   2007   NUMBER 2

© 2007 Lawrence & Wishart
99a Wallis Road, London E9 5LN
Email: lw@l-w-bks.demon.co.uk
Tel: 020 8533 2506

ISSN 0967 3393

Cover illustration: © Luis Jacob, courtesy of Brich Libralato, Toronto
'A Dance for Those of Us Whose Hearts Have Turned to Ice, based on the
choreography of Françoise Sullivan and the sculpture of Barbara Hepworth
(with Sign-Language Supplement)', 2007; still from video installation.

Peruvian-Canadian artist Luis Jacob has been involved in the Toronto
anarchist milieu for many years. In the summer of 1998 he helped found
the Toronto Anarchist Free School (1998-2001), and he has participated in
the Free School's successor, Anarchist U (2003-present). In addition to his
activism, Jacob is an artist and curator who has mounted a number of
exhibitions related to Queer culture (notably 'Out of the Showers and Into
the Streets: Remembering the Bathhouse Raids', Art Metropole, Toronto
2001, and 'The JDs Years: 1980s Queer Zine Culture from Toronto', Art
Metropole, Toronto and Helen Pitt Gallery, Vancouver 1999). As his
politics evolve, so too does his art. 'A Dance for Those of Us Whose
Hearts Have Turned to Ice' includes a pamphlet of quotations by anarchist
artists and critics and caused a sensation this summer at Europe's
preeminent contemporary art exhibition, Documenta 12.

Allan Antliff

ANARCHIST STUDIES: PAST, PRESENT AND FUTURE

By coincidence, both Jon Purkis and I will be resigning our posts in *Anarchist Studies* after this issue: Ruth Kinna will then become editor, and Dave Berry will be book reviews editor. This will, inevitably, lead to some changes in the journal, and so it seems a good moment to review progress so far, and to consider the way ahead. This section groups together some texts by people who have been involved with *Anarchist Studies* for many years: their judgements and opinions are not being presented as definitive rulings, and I know that Ruth will welcome any feedback or commentaries on these ideas.

Back in 1997 I was surprised and delighted to realize that *Anarchist Studies* had reached its fifth year. Ten years later, it is still developing, and I hope it's still interesting and relevant.

Sharif Gemie

A brief history of *Anarchist Studies* (so far)

LEWIS CALL

For the past fifteen years, AS has been many things: innovative, insightful, provocative, occasionally outrageous – but never boring! AK Press has called *Anarchist Studies* 'the premier scholarly journal on anarchism ... erudite, and informed.'[1] AS provokes strong feelings, pro and con – surely a sign of success for any anarchist publication. Reviewing the AS archive, one is struck by the remarkable consistency of what we may perhaps call the *Anarchist Studies* project. Since its inception, the journal has consistently attempted to broaden the scope of anarchist discourse by introducing themes, topics, perspectives and methodologies which have not traditionally been considered relevant to anarchism. This essay will examine that ambitious attempt, paying particular attention to the ways in which AS has tried to make anarchism more theoretically sophisticated, more green, more international, and more applicable to the political conditions which obtain in the era of fully globalised capital.

Anarchist Studies arrived with a bang in the spring of 1993. The first issue featured a lead article on anarcho-syndicalism by Murray Bookchin, who was by then one of the international anarchist community's best known intellectuals. From the very beginning, however, it was apparent that AS would do much more than simply publish and discuss the pronouncements of anarchism's 'great men' (though the journal would always continue to offer intriguing interpretations and re-assessments of Godwin, Kropotkin, Bakunin, Stirner, Chomsky, Bookchin, etc.). Thus the first issue also featured a piece on Wilhelm Reich and sexuality in the Spanish Revolution by Richard Cleminson, and a look at the anarchist art of John Cage, by Richard Kostelanetz. In his editorial introduction to the second issue, Tom Cahill made the desire for innovation explicit: 'We might be bold about it and claim to be part of an effort to re-define what is central and what is marginal.' The underlying objective was perhaps a bit hazy at first, but it would gradually become clearer as the journal grew and matured: the idea was to build new forms of anarchist thinking, criticism and politics which would update the received traditions of 'classical' anarchism, in order to make anarchism more meaningful and relevant in the postmodern period.

When Tom was forced to step down as editor due to a kidney transplant in 1995, Sharif Gemie took the editor's chair ('an attractive piece of furniture' with 'a few distinctive bumps and scratches,' he joked in AS 3:1). Sharif made it clear that he would continue to nurture the creative, experimental spirit which had already become such an important part of AS: 'One of the most encouraging signs is that a distinct "AS style" seems to be emerging: one that is at once sympathetic to but also critical of the anarchist tradition,' he wrote in his first editorial (AS 3:1).

Sharif set an ambitious agenda: more articles about sexual politics, more on anarchism and post-modernity, more 'green' articles, more on the Third World. The journal's diverse collection of contributors would deliver. AS 4:1 brought an important account of 'free love' in Imperial Germany by Hubert van den Berg. AS 4:2 featured a groundbreaking piece on 'Anarchy on the Internet' by Chris Atton. When this article appeared in October 1996, the Internet had been around for about thirteen years (and had been well-known for much less time), and the World Wide Web was still a relatively recent invention. But as Atton made clear, anarchists already understood how this technology could dramatically expand the opportunities for alternative electronic publishing.

By 1996, the anarchist community had begun to view AS as a major site of intellectual discussion and (in the best sense of the word) argument. The Debate section was introduced in AS 4:2; it featured a lively, energetic encounter between L. Susan Brown and Janet Biehl, based upon Bookchin's critique of Brown's work in *Social Anarchism or Lifestyle Anarchism*. AS 5:1 included debate about van den Berg's article. AS 6:1 offered a debate about Paul Nursey-Bray's reading of Godwin (which had appeared in AS 4:2). AS 6:1 also contained my first contribution to the journal, an attempt to re-read early modern political philosopher John Locke as a proto-anarchist. I was a young graduate student when I wrote this piece; how delighted I was when I received AS 7:1 (March 1999) and saw Dave Morland and Terry Hopton's sophisticated 'Locke and Anarchism: A Reply to Call.' I had never imagined that anyone might find my work important enough to challenge. Suddenly I felt that I was part of something larger, a vibrant intellectual community that cherishes the tradition of civilized intellectual debate which stretches all the way back to the ancient Greek city-states.

AS has published papers on a remarkably diverse array of topics over the past fifteen years. Still, certain general trends have emerged. For example, AS has always recognized the vital role which postmodernism and post-structuralism play in contemporary debates about anarchist theory. By no means has AS provided an uncritical endorsement of the various 'post-' theories. Instead, the journal has consistently offered a stimulating conversation about the relevance (or irrelevance) of these theories to contemporary anarchism. In AS 5:2 (October 1997), Andrew M. Koch considered the possibility that Max Stirner may have been the first poststructuralist, while John Moore offered a review article on anarchism and poststructuralism. In October 1999, John (now Associate Editor) guest-edited a special issue of AS on Anarchism and Science Fiction. In his editorial introduction, John made explicit the intriguing connections between anarchism, postmodernism and science fiction, citing the work of political philosopher Todd May and that of American SF writer/critic Samuel Delany. I was happy to see my essay on postmodern anarchism in the novels of William Gibson and Bruce Sterling appear alongside excellent anarchist readings of Pat Murphy, Joan Slonczewski, Eric Frank Russell and Star Trek's Borg. AS 8:1 featured a sophisticated review essay by Karen Goaman and Mo Dodson on Habermas and the postmodern turn. Saul Newman, who is now a leading figure in the growing field of 'post-anarchism,' has continued to develop the poststructuralist reading of anarchism, offering a very thought-provoking piece on Stirner and Deleuze in AS 9:2, as well as a stimulating paper on anarchism, Marxism and Bonapartism in AS 12:1.

The journal's commitment to a theoretically sophisticated anarchist discourse is very deep, and that commitment is not limited to those theories whose names begin with 'post-'. AS has also consistently insisted that anarchism must address the concerns of feminists and gender theorists. The connection between anarchism and feminism is not a new one; certainly anarchists have recognized this connection since the days of Emma Goldman. (Goldman herself has drawn the attention of several AS contributors: Cliff Hawkins looked at her views on political violence in AS 7:1, while Jim Jose assessed her contribution to anarchist theory in AS 13:1.) However, AS has done quite a bit to strengthen, expand and radicalize the anarcho-feminist connection. In AS 3:2, Val Plumwood examined issues of privacy from an anarchist feminist perspective. Hélène Bowen Raddeker offered a fascinating look at Japanese anarcho-feminist Ito Noe in AS 9:2. The journal's commitment to anarcho-feminism has been part of a broader attempt to ensure that anarchists will take seriously issues of gender and sexuality. Richard Cleminson, who has been a regular contributor to the journal since the beginning and an Associate Editor since 1998, has done a great deal to move this project forward. In AS

5:1, Richard continued to explore the theories of sexuality which developed among the Spanish anarchists, focusing this time on Félix Martí Ibáñez. In October 2000, Richard guest-edited another special issue of AS, this one on Anarchism and Sexuality. As he observed in his editorial introduction, AS 8:2 demonstrated 'the extremely diverse set of interventions that anarchists in one shape or another have made to tackling sexuality and gender in different countries over time.' This issue featured essays on a breathtakingly broad array of topics, including sexuality in the Spanish Civil War, anarchist discourses on masturbation, the sexual revolution in 1960s Germany, and even a discussion of anarchism and the Marquis de Sade. More recently, the journal has begun to explore the intersection of anarchism and queer theory. Aaron Lakoff's interview with Yossi represented an initial exploration of the vital connections between anarchism and radical queer culture (AS 13:2). The theoretical terrain surrounding 'queer anarchism' appears to be very rich indeed, and I hope that we will see more work on this important topic in the future.

Those of us who have been following AS for some time remember with fondness the journal's old black and red covers – very traditional, very 'old school' and, until 1996, quite devoid of graphics! However, a journal as subversive as AS could hardly remain content to promote the colours of 'classical' anarchism alone. In retrospect, it is not surprising that the journal developed what Tom Cahill called a 'green tinge' (AS 2:2). In his Autumn 1994 editorial, Tom argued that 'the environmental movement would benefit greatly from a bit more anarchist input.' I would only add that the reverse is also true: anarchism has benefited greatly from its encounter with environmentalism. AS 2:2 featured an important piece on sustainable development by Glenn Albrecht, and an insightful look at Peter Marshall's 'libertarian ecology' by John Clark. The review section in that issue focused heavily on green themes, and the journal's book reviewers would continue to discuss green politics, ecology, urban planning, etc. In its green moments, the journal has managed to escape briefly from its ivory tower and focus on 'real world' social and political movements. Examples of this phenomenon include Ian Welsh and Phil McLeish's piece on anarchist opposition to the UK Roads Programme (AS 4:1), Chris Atton's study of the *Green Anarchist* newspaper (AS 7:1), and Ben Lawley's look at ecological libertarianism in the UK Social Housing Development (AS 9:1). Although the journal has remained comfortable in its academic 'niche,' pieces such as these have ensured that AS would also remain relevant to practicing non-academic anarchists. AS 12:1 featured two papers on ecology: Viktor Postnikov's study of ecological thinking in nineteenth-century Russia, and Robert Graham's provocative critique of social ecology. (The latter piece proved so controversial that it was still provoking debate late in 2006; AS 14:2 featured a spirited exchange between Graham and John Clark.) I am confident that AS will continue to insist that the proper colours of twenty-first century anarchism must surely be black, red and green.

Anarchist Studies has always tried to move the anarchist discourse beyond its European origins. AS 6:2 featured a remarkable article by John A. Rapp on the connections between Daoism and anarchism. By this time (1998), AS had already run several articles on Asian anarchism, including Mihara Yoko's 'Anarchism in Japan' (AS 1:2) and John Crump's 'Anarchism and Nationalism in East Asia' (AS 4:1). In his editorial for AS 8:1 (March 2000), Sharif Gemie spoke admiringly of Rapp's paper on Daoism, and invited readers to submit 'essays on the Islamic contribution to anarchism.' He thus identified what was, at the time, a major lacuna in AS: although the journal had done groundbreaking work on Asian anarchism, there had not yet been anything on anarchism in the Islamic or Arab worlds. The fascination with Asia continued with Rapp's work on Maoism and anarchism (AS 9:1), and Raddeker's piece on Ito Noe (AS 9:2), but it was not until 2002 that AS explicitly took up the question of anarchism in the Islamic world. No doubt this move was partly inspired by the events of 11 September 2001. In Spring 2002, AS published a timely, relevant 'round table' discussion on 'Anarchism after 11 September.' Contributors included AS regulars Sharif Gemie, Ronald Creagh and Karen Goaman, German commentator Johannes von Hösel, anarchist groups from Fraga and Istanbul, and world famous 'libertarian socialist' Noam Chomsky. This discussion provided badly needed historical and political context which helped to demystify the terrorist attacks; it thus represented a valuable antidote to the reductionist 'with us or against us' rhetoric of Bush and his cheerleaders in the mainstream media. In an important contribution to AS 10:2, Harold B. Barclay explored a 'possible relationship between the idea of anarchy and Muslim society.' Georges Rivière studied anarchist movements in Algeria in AS 11:2. AS 13:1 featured an indispensable discussion of 'The Torture Show – Reflections on Iraq and the West,' with contributions from Sharif Gemie, Allan Antliff and Marcus Milwright, and the prominent Turkish anarchist Sureyyya Evran. AS 14:1 consisted mainly of an extended debate surrounding the French government's controversial decision to ban 'ostentatious' religious symbols – specifically, the Muslim veil – in French state schools. Sharif Gemie's insightful paper criticized the positive response of the French anarchist journal *Monde Libertaire* to this provocative ban, and numerous contributors commented and expanded upon Sharif's work.

For the past five years or so, AS has been focused – quite rightly, in my view – on the problems and perils of what we now call 'globalisation.' In their 2003 guest editorial, Ian Welsh and Jon Purkis argued compellingly that in the present situation, unfettered global capital is a far more dangerous force than the nation state, which does occasionally provide 'critical bulwarks against the worst excesses of global corporations operating within a deregulated market system' (AS 11:1).[2] (The fascination with post-structuralism also remained in evidence; Ian and Jon proved conclusively that no guest editorial is complete without a reference to the work of Todd May.) Continuing the theme that has guided AS since its creation, Ian and Jon called for a 'diversity of engagement' which would not be embodied in any one particular form. This emphasis on the diversity of tactics and forms was exemplified by Allan Antliff's remarkable analysis of anarchist art, which built upon the work of the late John Moore, whose obituary appeared in the same issue (AS 11:1). Alan O'Connor's sophisticated piece on Mexican anarcho-punk continued this trend in the following issue, which also featured Karen Goaman's thoughtful paper on carnivalesque symbolic action in the anti-globilisation movement, held over from the overflowing AS 11:1. Interest in the issues of the global economy was so extensive that AS 12:1 featured a debate section on 'Anarchism and Globalisation.' Gavin Grindon continued the exploration of carnival's radical potential in AS 12:2, which also featured a look at anarchist modernism in Argentinian literature by Glen S. Close. In an ambitious paper in AS 14:2, Linden Farrer explicitly tied resistance to the G8 to post-structuralist anarchism, thus bringing together two major concerns of AS.

I would be remiss if I did not emphasize the importance of AS's remarkable book review section. Under the stalwart leadership of Carl Levy (from 1993 through 2001) and Jon Purkis (from 2002 until quite recently), *Anarchist Studies* has published thought-provoking reviews on a broad range of anarchist literature. The book review forum has always been a feisty, energetic section of AS. Not content to accept its given place in the back pages of the journal, the book review section has, from time to time, challenged and subverted the privileged position of the 'feature articles' – in the finest anarchist tradition! My understanding of the literature by, about, and of interest to anarchists has been greatly enhanced by these reviews and review essays. I am especially grateful for the frequent contributions of Brian Morris, Colin Ward, David Goodway, John Crump, Ruth Kinna, Karen Goaman and John Moore.

Where do we go from here? I hope that we will continue the project which began fifteen years ago, for that project is by no means complete. There are still anarchist stories which remain untold. For example, anarchists have not yet really dealt with the full implications of the insurgency which anarchism is currently conducting inside popular culture. Anarchism has become remarkably fashionable of late, and is depicted in mainstream culture in ways that are surprisingly positive. What are we to make of the amazing popularity of *V for Vendetta*, Alan Moore's grim vision of a near-future totalitarian England, in which would-be 17th century 'terrorist' Guy Fawkes is not burned in annual effigy, but celebrated as a freedom fighter? In the hands of Hollywood's sometimes brilliant Wachowski brothers, *V for Vendetta* has been ably translated into a striking critique of Anglo-American politics in the post-9/11 world. What does it mean that, at a time when the forces of capitalism and imperialism seem more oppressively powerful than ever, popular culture can provide such positive anarchist narratives?

Anarchist Studies has come a long way over the past decade and a half. The journal has had two publishers. The move from Cambridge's White Horse

Press to London's Lawrence and Wishart in 2002 brought a smaller trim size, full colour covers (purists remain sceptical about the higher production values!) and modest opportunities for increased circulation. The journal has had two editors so far. I am grateful to Tom Cahill for getting the journal started in the first place, and to Sharif Gemie for a decade of hard work which has helped make AS into what it is today: one of the foremost fora for the serious discussion of anarchist theory and practice. I would also like to ask all AS readers to join me in welcoming our new editor, longtime AS contributor and Associate Editor Ruth Kinna.

And what about this 'brief history?' Has it been too celebratory? Probably. A journal which features the word 'anarchist' in its name has been in continuous publication for the past fifteen years, and shows no signs of stopping. In my book, that is cause for celebration. Are there aspects of the journal's history which should be approached with a more critical eye? Perhaps, but I leave that for the next history, and the next historian. Diversity of engagement means, among other things, that there are as many versions of *Anarchist Studies* as there are readers of *Anarchist Studies*. So come on, all you cyborgs and Situationists, you ecologists and egoists, you punks and perverts. Who will narrate the next version?

NOTES

1. *AK Press*. Accessed 30 July 2007. <http://www.akpress.org/2007/items/anarchist-studiestwelvetwo>

2. Noam Chomsky has made a similar argument: 'My short-term goals are to defend and even strengthen elements of state authority which, though illegitimate in fundamental ways, are critically necessary right now to impede the dedicated efforts to 'roll back' the progress that has been achieved in extending democracy and human rights. State authority is now under severe attack in the more democratic societies, but not because it conflicts with the libertarian vision. Rather the opposite: because it offers (weak) protection to some aspects of that vision.' *Powers and Prospects*, Boston: South End Press, 1996, p. 73-74.

Anarchist theory: what should be done?

BRIAN MARTIN

Where is anarchist theory going? Where *should* it be going?

It's useful to make a comparison with other bodies of theory. Marxism and feminism spring to mind. Despite the collapse of socialist states, Marxism remains influential among scholars, among whom the study of Marx's works continues to play a big role. Anarchism shares with Marxism a preoccupation with classic theorists – for Marx and Engels substitute Bakunin and Kropotkin

– but anarchism has never had anything like the scholarly attention or intellectual commitment inspired by Marxism.

Feminism remains a vibrant theoretical enterprise, drawing on a variety of thinkers. Once again, anarchism has received far less scholarly attention.

Both Marxism and feminism were inspired by, and inspired, social movements. Each has developed esoteric theoretical branches, largely restricted to scholars (and maybe their students) and separate from the day-to-day concerns of activists. Anarchism has not had a theoretical wing of similar scale or exclusiveness.

In a narrow sense, anarchism can refer to a critique of the state and to anti-state practice. In a broader sense, it can refer to a critique of domination – incorporating a critique of the state plus critiques of capitalism, patriarchy, racism and other oppressive systems – and associated practices. Anarchists seldom try to impose an anti-state lens on all forms of oppression. But few Marxists and feminists are one-dimensional either.

More than other forms of critique, anarchism contains a vision of an alternative – a self-managing society – and preferred means for achieving it, namely a practice that reflects the goal. This is unlike Marxism, in which the ultimate goal of communism, a society without the state, has never been well articulated, and in which the means are justified by the ends: capturing state power is the means to achieve stateless communism. Feminists subscribe to an ideal of gender equality, but this has many versions, from anarcha-feminist visions to a hierarchical society in which women hold just as many positions of power as men. Feminists differ considerably concerning the means to achieve their ideals.

If social goals and methods play a large role in the anarchist project, what does this say about anarchist theory? Should scholarship be dismissed as elitist and therefore incompatible, as a means, with the goal of an egalitarian society? This doesn't make sense, at least in the short term, because anarchist practice needs critical scrutiny, like any other practice. But are there ways to supplement conventional modes of scholarly production?

Anarchists point to a long tradition of radical education, including schools in which teachers and learners make decisions collectively. Modes of decision-making are a key part of what is often called the hidden curriculum, namely the things learned through the structure of the educational process rather than the formal things studied. Egalitarian education suggests a different process for producing and using theory.

There is also a tradition of activist learning and teaching, especially in times of oppression, social crisis or revolution, such as teach-ins against wars and learning within opposition movements. However, this does not seem to have had much effect on the content of what is learned, nor has it given rise to sustained alternative modes of intellectual production.

Inspiration can be drawn from the new mode of network production, used in creating free software through voluntary contributions managed by an individual or small group, and extended to other domains, most prominently wikipedia. How this could be adapted to intellectual work in more traditional areas remains to be seen.

Activist groups occasionally have adopted an extreme ethos of egalitarianism, making the assumption that everyone can develop the full range of skills needed in the group, everything from organising events, dealing with disputes and public speaking. This is commendable when it empowers members who might otherwise be stuck with less attractive tasks, but it may inhibit advanced intellectual work.

Studies of expertise show that many years of persistent practice and training are needed to make world-class contributions. Surely this applies to developing new anarchist theory. Yet becoming a talented theorist should not – according to anarchist ideals – lead to any special privileges. Managing the tension between expertise and egalitarianism is an important task for anarchists. The existence of this tension may help explain why anarchism has had such a low profile among scholars.

What sort of theory should be developed? One possibility is a high-level, grand theory of domination, oppression, inequality and/or hierarchy. It would bring together, or supersede, separate critiques of capitalism, patriarchy, the state and other oppressive systems. Anarchists have long been eclectic, freely drawing on other critiques, such as the Marxist analysis of capitalism. A grand theory of domination would be a specific anarchist contribution.

Another possibility is a high-level, grand theory of anarchist alternatives, providing the general conditions for and constraints on a society built around equality, solidarity and freedom. The alternative might be a single model or a set of plural, diverse self-managing societies. The theory might be centred on the alternative structures or it might focus on self-organisation, namely the process for creating and maintaining desirable alternatives.

Another opening for anarchist theory is addressing particular topics aside from traditional ones such as the state, education, and workers' self-management. Possibilities include bureaucracy, communication, defence and technology. Anarchist perspectives have little visibility in these areas.

Anarchist theory might also address personal and interpersonal dynamics, such as self-understanding, commitment, happiness, friendship and solidarity. Such issues are important in their own right and have connections to big-picture approaches to politics and economics.

Finally, there is meta-theory: an anarchist theory of theory, including an anarchist theory about anarchist theory. What is the role of theory in the anarchist project? Should theory include both simple and complex facets and, if so, how should the complex aspects relate to the simple bits? How and to what extent can theory become a collective project, linked with practice? Is there a simple way to learn how to develop theory, so that lots of people can join in?

There's certainly plenty to do!

Facilitating diversity
Some thoughts on being a book reviews editor

JON PURKIS

This is my last issue of the journal as the Book Reviews Editor and I would like to use this as an opportunity to say thank you to everyone who has worked with me during this time, whether it has been writing a review, recommending a reviewer, or making suggestions about possible reviews in the future. I'd also like to apologise to those people who I said that I'd get a book for and didn't: perhaps it was my fault, perhaps it was the publisher's! I would also like to make a number of observations about the ethics of reviewing (and also being a reviewer), prompted by my experience, but also because I think that these matters are under-discussed generally.

A starting point for this might be the hope that after five years of commissioning and editing book reviews for *Anarchist Studies*, readers were no less the wiser about my own anarchist politics and interests. Obviously, I have been involved in anarchist activism and academia too long for this to be the case, but one of the responsibilities of being a reviews editor is surely to try and represent the range of ideas within the field as much as is possible.

One may not always see the reviews editor as being a political position, but the selection of texts can create a feel for what the journal is about as much as the actual full length articles. Irrespective of which texts one actually 'commissions' (and of course there is no guarantee that they will appear anyway), every issue of *Anarchist Studies* creates its own special dilemma about the content that one is sent. How fair am I being to particular reviewers based on their observance of deadlines, their writing style or their experience? Does the order of the reviews favour a particular person? Should I call any of the submissions a 'review article' and therefore earn the reviewer some small status on their publications curriculum vitae?

In the context of a relatively low circulation journal these might seem needlessly trivial and obvious matters, but there are points of principle here, as with anything that involves working with other writers, researchers and their egos. There needs to be something of a consistency about how an editor deals with their reviewer as much as how the reviewer deals with the subject of their chosen text. Nobody wants to be told that they are a poor reviewer or that their writing style is amateurish, just as we as researchers despise the vindictive reviewer who apparently ignores the bulk of our work in order to exaggerate one particular grievance. Thus any anarchist involved in an editing process should always seek to empower rather than belittle the contributor, even if this involves considerable effort on their part.

Such ethical dilemmas are even more pertinent in an age where we deal with so many people through the medium of email, rarely resorting to the relative transparency of the telephone conversation. Approximately fifty per cent of the people that I have liased with as reviews editor I have never met and would probably walk past in the street. Fortunately, the sense of trust generated by a common purpose has overcome some of the limitations of virtual forms of communication.

Of course this must work the other way as well; reviewers have responsibilities too, and whilst we all have a few unreviewed texts propping open the door, it is simply a matter of admitting that a task is beyond us and letting the reviews editor know this (particularly when there are pushy publishers around!)

As a general point, I do look forward to the time when the sense of common purpose which has largely been my experience of being a reviews editor, also extends across more geographical boundaries and we begin to recruit more reviewers and writers from outside the Western anarchist axis of North America, Europe and Australia. However, there is a healthy turnover of new reviewers coming to the fore, some of whom are not 'official' scholars, but who bring their practical experiences of protest, of education, music and so forth to their critical work. This means that the journal may include reviews which are not exclusively 'about' anarchism but are penned by anarchists striving to generate more debate about anarchist concerns (see James Bowen's review in this volume). This also adds to the feel of *Anarchist Studies* being a little bit different to other journals, with a slightly looser remit of study (see 'Anarchist Studies and the Community of Scholars' in Volume 12 (1)).

I would certainly extend that analogy in terms of broadening the 'book' reviews section to something that might look a little more multi-media on occasion. After all, anarchist scholarship is now very well established in cyberspace and engagement with the electronic presentation of information and opinion needs to be taken as seriously as anarchist theory and practice in book form. Similarly, anarchist publishers such as AK Press now regularly produce DVDs of speeches, essays, songs and poetry, many of which deserve attention. At the other end of the technological spectrum, I would like to see the efforts of the Kate Sharpley Library – who produce a constant stream of booklets about forgotten figures in anarchist history, including a decent proportion from South America – a bit more rewarded in terms of reviewer interest.

So, it's been a good experience and I wish my successor Dave Berry all the best, just as I am grateful to Carl Levy for setting the benchmark for so long. Here's to healthy reviewing in the future.

Such, such were the joys

Confessions of an anarcho-editorialist

SHARIF GEMIE

About twelve years ago, Tom Cahill asked me to consider becoming editor for *Anarchist Studies*. The initial proposal was that we should co-edit the journal, but it was clear that, given Tom's continuing and serious sickness, co-editorship would quickly become sole editorship. I had not been expecting any such invitation, and I can remember feeling very uncertain. I anticipated many possible problems and dilemmas: most of these worries have proved quite illusory, although there have been a number of other issues which did surprise and concern me. Today I'm in the position of passing on the now attractively distressed editorial chair to Ruth, and taking this opportunity to reflect on twelve years of my life.

Without doubt, it has been a positive experience. When Tom passed on the editor's position to me, *Anarchist Studies* had only been published for two years. For better or worse, I've been central to defining and developing an identity for the fledging child. One point has to be stressed here: editing a journal is not like commanding a battleship. The editor cannot call down 'now turn to the left'; he cannot pick up the phone to demand 'write me three papers on the labour movement: and remember to spell it with a "u"'. It's been more like flying a hot-air balloon: we can go up or down; we can make some sort of decision about whether the outlook is set fair, middling or stormy; but we can't – easily – change direction. I've tried hard to keep an open mind, and nudge the little craft towards some friendly harbours. I've read Lewis's potted history of the past fifteen years and – while I can certainly see the trends he's identified – I have to say that these weren't conscious policies.

If you google on *Anarchist Studies*, you quickly come across an interview with Ben Franks, in which the pseudonymous interviewer remarks that anarcho-academics don't seem to be doing much: there's just the 'strangely sombre' *Anarchist Studies*. [http://www.variant.randomstate.org/27texts/alliances27.html] When I first read this, I felt annoyed. But, as I thought about it further, I felt more relaxed. I suppose that if *Anarchist Studies* can be now be labelled with this easy cliché, then it is has become easily identifiable, and this can be seen as the achievement of some sort of success. Rather than 'strangely sombre', I prefer the review published in *Anarchy: A Journal of Desire Armed*, 23:2 (Fall 2005).

> This is an excellent, thoughtful and contentious anarchist publication. It represents the best of the academic anarchist press, engaging on a variety of issues, with a depth sorely needed by the milieu in general.

Let's be honest: *Anarchist Studies* is a good journal. The world's only anarcho-academic review. There are some fine competitors: *Social Anarchism* is a pleasant, relaxed read, with an attractive mixture of poetry, fiction, drawings and letters – but *Anarchist Studies* does better analyses and discussions. *Anarchy* has a massive circulation, an imaginative layout and its activist, polemical style is successful at drawing in a certain strand of militant youth – but AS is better at serious debate. *Réfractions* does some great papers, but its editorial style is inconsistent and the papers themselves are sometimes repetitive. *Democracy and Nature* promised a lot, but seems to have succumbed to the Fotopoulos syndrome, whereby every third footnote has to be a hymn of praise to the Great Editor. And so, gentle reader, our little baby has come to pull its weight. It's published some great articles which I think any journal of political or social debate would have been proud to publish. Perhaps more importantly, in almost every issue, there's usually been one article about which I've thought 'now where else could that have been published?' – a sign of the development of a genuine AS style.

My role in all this has been to make some rather limited decisions about style and scope. Occasionally outsiders seem to imagine that AS, a highly politicized journal, must be continually shaken by ferocious, political debates. It's actually been rather calm. In 1998, I decided that being editor on my own was rather lonely, and so I created the 'Associate Editors'. These supplemented the book review editor: I tend to think of them as the AS Editor's support group. Whenever there's been an awkward issue, I've sent round an e-mail and waited for pithy advice or at least sympathy. (John Moore was particularly effective in writing messages along the lines of 'well that's another fine mess you've got us into …') The nearest thing we ever had to a political debate was the discussion concerning the reactions to Carol Hamilton's guest editorial in AS 9:2 – about which, on reflection, I now consider I was entirely right. The simple truth is that we're just too small a grouping to consider strong disagreements, and therefore anyone involved in AS at any level has probably decided in advance that they may as well rub along with the others.

There have been a few bumps along the way: some turbulence, to revert to the hot air ballooning metaphor. One issue that has come up several times has been the idea of publishing less academic pieces. Some contributors are fixed on the idea that AS should publish ten thousand word essays, each with at least fifty footnotes and obligatory references to Foucault. Particularly after we moved to Lawrence and Wishart, which meant a switch to slightly more space, I've thought that we can afford to publish some short, un-footnoted, opinion pieces alongside the standard academic essay. I've always tried to judge each text on its own merits, rather than demanding a standard format. Hence the piece on *Anarchism Lancastrium* (AS 10.1) was accepted even though it's clearly not a sophisticated exercise in media studies, but rather a simple, eloquent piece of autobiographical writing. I'd still like to see a step or two towards a rather more varied selection of different styles of writing.

Another issue has been the famous 'right to reply'. This has also caused 'some turbulence'. I've come round to thinking that any contributor to AS has a 'right to reply' if, firstly, they raise substantial points and, secondly, if they keep their reply reasonably polite. Several writers have expected the right to defame, insult and publicly humiliate those who dared criticize them – described once as 'the glorious polemical style of the 1960s'. I still consider that this style of writing is extremely off-putting, and that it encourages personal feuds rather than genuine debate. For this reason, insults and name-calling have been edited out of all contributions.

Of course, there has been a problem with the famous 'Grumpy Old Men' of anarchism. This was not unexpected, and – like wind and rain – just has to be put up with it. (I firmly intend to grow more immature with age, and have promised Ruth that I will not become her GOM.)

The greatest problem of all, and probably my biggest disappointment, has been the overwhelming silence of the readership. As editor, I get very little feedback at all. Perhaps one or two comments a year. This has made me feel extremely uncertain about the role of the journal. One of the reasons for the so-called 'humorous' editorials was simply my own uncertainty about what to say to the silent masses. (Although I still like the science-fiction parody of AS 4:2 – not an original joke, but nonetheless a good one.) For anarchists, some of you are very passive, silent people.

The best moments, however, have been getting in contact with people I'd otherwise never have known. Many of the contributors have thanked me, which is pleasing. There are many, many people I'd like to name here: too many for this short note. But, in particular, I'd like thank Brian Martin, Lewis Call and L. Susan Brown: I've never met any of you face-to-face, but it's made me very happy to hear from you.

Okay, Ruth: the day is bright, the winds are fair although there's a possibility of turbulence over in the west, and the craft is straining at the ropes. Remember to take a thermos, some sandwiches and a coat (it can get cold up there). And a dictionary. And some binoculars. And a camera. Don't do anything stupid, but – also – don't play it safe. Have a good flight and a soft landing in twelve years. Me and Tom would like to come with you, but we're staying with the ground support team for the moment.

Epilogue

RUTH KINNA

Sharif has put me at the helm and gone below deck. Fortunately he's not drunk; nor has he thrown himself overboard. Still, my excitement at the prospect of editing AS is matched by growing periods of apprehension.

Sharif and Jon, Tom Cahill and Carl Levy before them, have done an excellent job in establishing and sustaining the journal. It's clear from Lewis Call's review that AS has published some outstanding work, that it has shown an admirable openness to research in the field and that it has a growing reputation for tackling messy and difficult issues. *Anarchy: A Journal of Desire Armed* has this to say about issue 14.2:

> *Anarchist Studies* continues to be one of the great contemporary anarchist periodicals. This issue demonstrates a trend that is lacking in North America: critical engagement. The French anarchist periodical *Le Monde Libertaire* more or less came out in support of the French state's ban on religious symbols (read: veils) in schools and this issue of *Anarchist Studies* is a series of ten introductions, essays, responses, and afterwords on the topic. At the heart of the issue is a certain kind of anarchist calculus. What does an anarchist reject first, the state or religion? Fascinating discussions that demonstrate how much better educated the Europeans are (with the caveat that most of the authors are hired intellectual thugs).[1]

It would be nice to maintain and build on this reputation. How? Tom Cahill gave the answers in issue 1. I plagiarize freely:

The success of AS depends on two things: first, the range and quality of the material submitted and second, a willingness to engage in constructive debate. Looking back on the past, it's of course possible to detect trends, but it's a mistake to think that these add up to a policy. If your interests or concerns have not been represented, then it's time you sent in a paper or even a proposal for an issue. AS is a peer reviewed journal which publishes the results of serious intellectual work (another of Tom's phrases) but contributors are not required to wear gowns and mortar boards or to produce references from employers. There is no requirement to submit 10,000 word articles; I draw the line at power-point slides but the guest editorial slot pioneered by Sharif provides space for short commentaries and these are also welcome. Equally, if you want to comment on a published piece, send in your response. There is, I think, a reasonable expectation that debates are conducted in a civil fashion, but full and frank disagreement is allowed.

So, in taking the wheel, I'm not attempting to chart a new course (too busy murdering metaphors).

Not Jack Sparrow, not Ahab. Call me Ishmael.

NOTES

1. *Anarchy: A Journal of Desire Armed*, 64 (2007), p.58.

What is anarchist literary theory?

JESSE COHN

Department of English and Modern Languages
Purdue University North Central
1401 S. U.S. Hwy. 421
Westville, IN 46391
jcohn@pnc.edu

ABSTRACT

Over the course of its history, the anarchist movement has produced a form of literary theory – a critical aesthetics and epistemology grounded in its emancipatory ethics. In sketching an outline of this body of thought, this essay attempts to call attention to several aspects which offer a promising alternative to the sterility of the modes of theory dominant within the academy.

1.

The recent revival of academic interest in the anarchist tradition has drawn new attention to its reflections in literature, particularly via the influence of the anarchist movement on avant-garde modernisms (e.g., Pound's poetry, Picasso's collages), and via the role played by figures of 'the anarchist' and 'anarchy' in certain narratives (e.g., Joseph Conrad's *The Secret Agent* or Frank Norris's *The Octopus*).[1] However, this discussion has all but entirely omitted any consideration of the possible contributions of anarchism to literary criticism. As Roger Dadoun writes, this contribution is not simply a matter of cataloging 'anarchist elements in literature,' whether works by anarchist authors, addressing anarchist topics, or purporting to be stylistically anarchic (1997, translation mine). Nor is a coherent body of anarchist theorization on literature a mere hypothesis; it exists, albeit almost completely consigned to official oblivion, in the historical archives. Like other forms of literary theory which draw on the traditions of oppositional political movements, e.g., ecocriticism, postcolonialism, marxism, feminism, queer theory, etc., anarchist literary theory draws its inspiration from the body of thought and practices which have historically comprised the anarchist movement.

2.

This tradition is manifold and still evolving; one can trace at least two major lines of development in anarchist theory, one of which leads from

Proudhon and Bakunin to Noam Chomsky and the late Murray Bookchin, the other stemming primarily from Max Stirner and coming, by several twists and turns, to influence Raoul Vaneigem, Fredy Perlman, and John Zerzan. The latter tendency, sometimes identified as 'individualist,' 'anti-organizationalist,' or 'primitivist,' has typically attracted a minority, although it now exercises a wider appeal for North American activists; the former, bearing stronger historical ties to the workers' movements of Europe and the Americas, is generally called 'social anarchism.' I will confine my generalizations to the majority tendencies of social anarchism, which have received far less attention in academic scholarship, but which have, I believe, far more to offer to a conversation about literary theory which has wandered into a kind of dead end.[2]

3.

A distinctive feature of anarchism, as a political movement, is that it roots itself not in a fixed epistemological schema, e.g., a set of propositions about the true structure of history, capital, patriarchy, etc., but in an ethical stance, the positive side of which consists in a fundamental affirmation of freedom, equality, and the coexistence of the different not only as *ends* but as *means*, the negative side of which consists in a fundamental refusal of domination and hierarchy per se, not only as instanced in relations of class *or* gender *or* race, etc., but in *any* and *all* relationship (Graeber 2004a:5-6; Granier I.3.3B, translation mine).

Anarchists oppose domination *as such,* not only insofar as this presents itself as the effect or byproduct of some supposedly fundamental category: 'Slavery may change its form or its name – its essence remains the same' (Bakunin 1972: 137). Thus, from the time of Proudhon on, anarchists have regarded not only Capital, the State, and the Church as analogous enemies (with overlapping interests), but also patriarchy, racism, colonialism, heterosexism, and so on, on the same *ethical grounds* (Colson 2001: 24, translation mine). Marxist theory presents itself as 'science' – as an 'analytical discourse' which describes how history progresses, or how capital works, or how class society is structured (Graeber 2004a: 6). By contrast, as Daniel Colson remarks, anarchist theory 'is above all an ethical project which directly engages, in its least practice, in judging the value of relations and situations' (2001: 108, translation mine; May and Lance 983-84). This ethics refuses to locate the desired good in some utopian elsewhere or elsewhen, in the afterlife or after the revolution, a deferral which authorizes the dualism of 'ends' versus 'means' (and, as Colson notes, 'the mastery over time that this distinction presupposes') but insists that means contain their own ends, that a genuinely transformative movement 'prefigures' the society it seeks to bring about in its practices here and now (Landauer quoted. in Lunn 1973: 227; Colson 2001: 119, translation mine; Graeber 2002: 62).

4.

This means that we do not need to approach any given text armed with predetermined categories that we read it against – e.g., the categories of class, gender, race, etc.; instead, we seek to enter a dialogue with the text, not only to critique it from an external perspective seen as superior, but to reconstruct our perspective with the aid of the text itself.

Herbert Read protested against the project of New Criticism, not only for its formalism but for its instauration of interpretive 'canons' which reduce each particular encounter between reader and text to an instance of the same ('turning every poem into a well-wrought urn or verbal icon according to these critics' special dicta,' as Valentine Cunningham puts it), an exercise in 'false method': 'the critical faculty, elaborating its laws too far from its immediate object, may construct categories or ideals that are in the nature of impassive moulds. The critic then returns to the plastic substance of art and in a moment, in the name of science, he has presented us with a rigid shape which he would persuade us is the living reality' (Cunningham 2002: 2; Read 1967: 37). This deductive model of inquiry is directly analogous to the vanguardist model of political action, in which the revolutionary élite, possessing 'correct' theory, imposes this rigid schema upon a 'mass' conceived as essentially homogenous and passive. By contrast, as Voline puts it, anarchists refuse to locate an ordering 'principle' in 'a centre *created in advance* to capture the whole and impose itself upon it,' seeking instead an order which emerges 'from all sides' (quoted in Guérin 1970: 43, italics mine). In this sense, anarchist inquiry refuses, as Kenneth Burke would put it, to read texts against 'a "symbolist dictionary" *already written in advance*'; it must be 'inductive,' always ready to rearticulate and reconstruct its own principles from inside the encounter with the text (Burke 1974: 89, italics mine; Jablon 1997: 1-2).

5.

For anarchists, treating literature as 'autonomous' from the social means failing to think autonomy in social terms; ergo, questions of literature must always be situated in a wider social context, with the aim of determining what kind of relationships the text offers to bring about between ourselves and one another, between ourselves and the world.

'Art,' declares an entry in the *Encyclopédie anarchiste*, 'must be *social* in the most complete sense of the word' (Faure 1934: 144). As Gustav Landauer put it, 'literature ... cannot be viewed as an autonomous activity,' separate from the rest of 'life,' without thereby falsifying it – indeed, not without fundamentally misconceiving the nature of autonomy, which is nothing if not a *social* relation: just as, for Bakunin, 'I am truly free only when all human beings, men and women, are equally free,' so we can conclude with Herbert Read that 'to escape from society (if that were possible) is to escape from the only soil rich enough to nourish art' (Lunn 1973: 44-45; Castoriadis 1998: 108; Bakunin 1972: 237; Read 1938: 20). Thus, for Ricardo Flores Magón, the very notion of 'art for art's sake' is 'an absurdity' (translation mine). Art cannot be removed to some 'mystical, transcendental sphere' outside of human relations; it must be 'situated,' created and received '*en situation*' (Litvak 1988: 76; Proudhon 1939: 276, 337). Like other 'signs,' literary texts in some sense 'help us to cope with their designates'; a 'style of speech' is also 'a way of being in the world' (Goodman 1971: 98). We are concerned with the *quality* of the various ways of being in the world that certain uses of language might afford us.

6.

At the same time, the particular text must never be simply reduced to an instance of a context, seen solely as the expression of some larger, fixed structure; there is always the possibility of surprise, of transformation.

If language were, in Nietzsche's phrase, an inescapable 'prison-house' (quoted in Jameson 1972: i), then there would be nothing for anarchists to do but surrender or be silent, which would amount to the same thing. However, this conception has never been accepted by anarchists such as Paul Goodman, who denounces it for 'abstracting language [*per se*],' i.e., what Saussure termed *la langue*, 'from speaking and hearing in actual situations,' i.e., concrete utterances, *la parole*, so as to privilege the 'constancy and supra-individuality' of language 'as against the variability and interpersonality of natural language' (1971: 86-87). Rather than 'take a statistical average of speech events and abstract a structure from it,' Goodman argues for a conception of 'language as the *tension* between the inherited code and what needs to be said,' a dynamic process rather than a static structure: 'the power to speak and hear continually modifies the code ... And language is not the code but these sentences' (1971: 137, 131, 33, italics mine).

In other words, for anarchists, language is not just the passive 'repetition of familiar signs' (Vaneigem 1994: 101); it is also an 'action' (Goodman 1964b: 248). Thus, writing and reading are not only the repeated confirmation of self-referential structures; they can be and are a means of *transformation* through which 'my preconceptions have been changed, I have been moved in ways that I had not expected' (1964b: 236).

Meanings are never simply 'reducible to the sum of the forces and elements which joined to produce them ... They are at the same time more and other, distinct from the forces which render them possible' (Colson 2004). Anarchist interpretation seeks both this ground of possibility and the possibilities themselves, the 'more and other.'

7.

Since an anarchist ethical stance means both a refusal to dominate and a refusal to be dominated, an ethical approach to the text cannot simply mean a receptive or empathetic reading, in which we merely submit to its terms, nor can it mean a purely active reading, reading as the 'use' or violent 'appropriation' of the text; instead of positing ourselves as the slaves or the masters of texts, we ought to place ourselves into a dynamic relation with them, to see each encounter with them as a dialogue fraught with risk and promise.

From one perspective, *interpretation* implies a cringing admission of 'indebtedness' to the text; rather than submit, the 'post-interpretive' reader declares that 'there is no longer an object to interpret,' or, as Stanley Fish and Richard Rorty suggest, that there is no 'text' which 'exist[s] independently of anything [the reader] might do' (Kristeva 1986: 306; Rorty 151; Fish 1980: 368). From another perspective, to *interpret* a text means 'to impose a limit on that text, to furnish it with a final signified, to close the writing' – 'an arbitrary imposition or a violent practice' (Barthes 1977: 147; Shapiro 1992: 2). From the first perspective, an anti-authoritarian interpretive practice would amount to resisting 'the tyranny of the signifier' in the name of the reader's 'freedom' (Owens 1983: 59; Culler 1983: 72); from the second perspective, an anti-authoritarian ethic would call for 'undermining ... the privileged status of the interpreter' (Spanos 1979: 135). The anarchist tradition suggests that both of these conceptions of freedom and interpretation are inadequate, and that only a dialogical conception will do.

For Proudhon, an anarchist discourse community is incompatible with the unquestioned supremacy of any fixed ideas, any 'absolute'; instead, it 'presupposes, as its principle, the greatest contradiction, and as its means, the greatest multiplicity possible' (1935: III.270, translation mine). Entering into this dialogue of many voices requires the participants to reframe their individual perspectives in terms of others', so that they progressively refine and break down 'their subjectivity, i.e. the absolute that the "me" affirms,' creating 'a common manner of seeing, which no longer resembles, either in content or in form, what it would have been without this debate ...' In short, the diversity and dissensus generated by perpetual discussion gives place to a 'new manner of seeing, constituted by relations which have been purged of metaphysical and absolutist elements,' which he calls 'the collective or public reason' (1935: III.256-61, translation mine).

This dialogue cannot take place, however, unless there is a genuine interplay between the parties involved. If I simply dominate the text, supplying all its meaning, then my perspective can never be changed or enriched by reading, and the 'me' remains (falsely) absolute; if I cannot contribute to the construction of meaning, however, then the text cannot tell me anything – unless, in fact, I substitute for the text as it exists, with all its possibilities, a preconceived interpretation, generally a received, traditional, rigidly conventional reading, as in the case of fundamentalist readings of the Torah, Bible, or Koran. In the latter case, I submit to the 'transcendent' authority of 'a vicariate, a priesthood ... [i.e., a] *Logos*'; in the former case, I enclose myself in a 'narcissism' or solipsism for which 'everything can be made up, finally nothing is given, there are no facts' (Dadoun 1997, translation mine; Proudhon 1935: III.363, translation mine; Goodman 1964b: 81). Only if the text and I can each contest one another, call one another into question, can there be an exercise of the 'collective reason' which permits freedom to coexist with community. Thus the necessity of a 'reading ... with double intent,' from perspectives which are internal to the text *and* from perspectives external to them, of reading with '*sympathy and empathy*' and of 'look[ing] for what hides *behind* discourses' (de Cleyre 1914: 379-380; Read 1967: 9; Granier 2003: II, 'Introduction,' translation mine). Through such a 'double labour,' we come not only to 'construct' the text that we 'apprehend,' but to 'respect' it, to allow it the opportunity to reconstruct ourselves: 'we make it at the same time that it makes us' (Dadoun 1997; Landauer 1974: 42, translations mine).

8.

The positive face of anarchism entails a theory of textual meaning *as* relationship – specifically, of textual meaning as that which emerges from two sets of relations: a.) the relations between the text and the forces which produced it within a given situation, and b.) the relations between the text *as* a force and its possible effects or uses in particular situations.

Since 'the fact and the idea are really inseparable,' it follows that we can interpret them: 'From all these facts, let us draw out the general idea' (Proudhon 1935: II.298, III.71, translation mine). This 'general idea' or 'logic of things' (Proudhon 1935: I.192, translation mine) can be thought in terms of a notion shared by Proudhon, Bakunin, and Kropotkin, namely, that of the 'resultant.' In Proudhon's words, 'everywhere there is a group, there is a resultant which is the power of the group, distinct not only from the particular forces or powers which compose the group, but also from their sum, and which expresses its synthetic unity, the pivotal, central function' (Proudhon 1935: III 408-409, translation mine). The relevant 'group,' in the case of a literary text, may include more than just the specific arrangement of signs on a specific number of pages; it may include the entire situation from which this arrangement emerged and any aspect of the changing situations in which a reader arrives at it. As Goodman emphasizes, an important dimension of meaning is 'the situation' of an utterance rather than its content, i.e., the *conditions* of 'the existence of the speech as an act': in the public rhetoric of politicians, for instance, 'the real meaning of the speeches, the goal of profits and power, is never stated' (1971: 97; 1964a: 65).

Textual meaning, from this perspective, is neither exclusive of nor limited to reference to an objectively existing reality ('within a spatial deployment of things and beings,' as Colson puts it); it includes the possibility of such reference within a wider conception of the text as an act, an event, a 'force' (2004: 152). Instead of isolating and privileging the purely performative aspect of signs – 'What is important in a text is not what it means, but what it does and incites to do' (Lyotard 1984: 9-10); 'language is the transmission of the word as order-word, not the communication of a sign as information' (Deleuze and Guattari 1987: 77) – anarchist theorizations of language refuse to 'hypostasize' the performative or the constative functions of language, and suggest that 'the two essential attributes of the same being,' are 'reason *and* force,' or 'signification and power': 'any force has a signification and ... any signification is the expression of a force' (Proudhon 1935: III.369; Colombo 2002: 132-133; Colson 2002: 144, translations mine). Moreover, each text, as an event, must be viewed both in retrospect, as the sequel to other events (other texts, the facts of the author's life, 'what they meant for them, in their time,' the cultural and historical milieu, even the objective referents which it may concern) *and* in prospect, as the possible cause of further and future events (other occasions, readings, receptions, and responses) (Landauer 1974: 50, translation mine). In this sense, the text is to be seen, no less than a human being, as 'at once a radically new, autonomous reality, carrying its own force, and at the same time the expression of the forces and powers which, in composing it, make it possible' (Colson 1998). It is possible, then, to regard texts as 'representations' of an objective world or 'expressions' of an author's subjectivity without thereby reducing them to these functions and without endorsing a naïve-realist theory of mimesis; it is also possible for an interpreter to claim to 'represent' the text without privileging a single, reductive reading.

9.

In this sense, then, anarchism is not simply a 'rejection of representation,' insofar as representation is synonymous with communication or meaning; for a text to fail to represent, communicate, or mean anything, it would have to have no relation to antecedents and no consequences, i.e., to be outside of all relationship, which is to say, to cease to be.

On the one hand, anarchism has always posed a rigorous and profound critique of the intersection of representation with power. So-called 'representative democracy,' from this perspective, is largely an apparatus for the transfer of power from the represented to the representative, a kind of floating signifier which can scarcely be adequate to the 'general will' which is its supposed signified. On the other hand, the alternative to the State is not a Rousseauvian 'state of nature,' a collection of absolutely self-contained individuals; it is the self-management of society. This self-management entails the establishment of a 'relationship' between people which *is* the adequate 'representation' of society by itself to itself: 'the government, no longer distinguishing itself from [our] interests and freedoms in so far as they place themselves in *relation* with one another, *ceases to exist*' (Proudhon 1936: 288-290, translation and italics mine). This relationship finds its forms in the horizontal *federation*, a 'forming and disbanding of thousands of representative, district, communal, regional, national bodies' which never subordinates the parts to the whole, and in the practice of *direct democracy*, whereby members of a collectivity assemble to formulate policy in person, sending *instructed* representatives (delegates) to convey their decisions to other bodies, empowered at any time 'to call them to order ... to replace them' (Malatesta 1993: 153; Leval 2005: 478). Rather than a static 'harmony,' then, anarchism produces a 'continually modified' series of arrangements, 'a temporary adjustment established among all forces acting upon a given spot ... representing every moment the resultant of all conflicting actions' (Kropotkin 1970: 121). While 'it is always an object of suspicion,' then, 'representation ... is thus not rejected *per se* by the anarchists'; it is not simply abolished but *reconceived* as plural and mobile (Granier 2003: II, 'Introduction,' translation mine).

This reconstruction of representation is implicit in the anarchist conception of freedom. Real emancipation, as opposed to formal or juridical right, for Bakunin, has to be conceived in social terms, not as independence from social relationships: 'The freedom of each individual is the ever-renewing result of numerous material, intellectual, and moral influences of the surrounding individuals and of the society into which he is born ... to wish to escape this influence in the name of a transcendental, divine, absolutely self-sufficient freedom is to condemn oneself to nonexistence' (1972: 257). To *be,* indeed, is to be 'grouped'; existence means 'collective being' (Proudhon 1946: 63, 80; 1935: III.263, translation mine). This collectivity cannot constitute itself, however, without communication and hence language: when 'language ... is lost,' André Léo writes, 'all that truly connects men and consolidates their relations' perishes with it. 'As a "structure of intelligibility" necessary to communication,' Caroline Granier elaborates, 'representation ensures the coherence of social exchanges: one could not reject it without attacking the social bond' (Léo quoted in Granier 2003: II, 'Introduction'; Granier 2003: II, 'Introduction,' translations mine). Thus understood, it quickly becomes apparent that, as Colson explains, although there is always a 'danger' that, if we fail to maintain a critical awareness of them, 'signs ... can come to substitute for the reality that they ought to *express,* to take their place,' i.e., that they can be reified into a new 'absolute,' they nonetheless 'play an essential role in the relations of "reciprocity" which the various collective beings are able to establish among themselves'; it is only *through* systems of signs, moreover, that 'collective beings not only have the possibility of increasing their power, but also, by associating with one another, of giving birth to much vaster collective beings endowed with a *collective reason*' (2001: 316).

10.

The primary critical question, for anarchists, is *how* a given text can be seen to represent *life.*

As an ethics that demands a 'continuous *evaluation* of the emancipatory or oppressive quality of actions, perspectives, and standpoints,' anarchism requires us to investigate 'their capacity (or lack thereof) to promote a stronger and freer *life*' (Colson 2001: 112, 299, translation and emphases mine). When we do so in the context of literary and cultural studies, we are guided by our critical understanding of language and its representational powers.

In his critique of structuralist linguistics, Goodman critiques 'the thesis of Benjamin Whorf, that the language determines the metaphysics of the tribe and what people can think,' arguing that 'language is checked by non-verbal experience,' that it is 'plastic' enough to '[say] new things,' and that we can and do 'communicate across the barrier of culture and language.' However, he suggests, 'if we put Whorf's thesis in a more modest form, it is more rewarding. People use language, they are not [merely] determined by it; but when they do use it – and by the language they choose – they focus their experience and define and limit their thoughts. A *style* of speech is an hypothesis about how the world is' (1971: 171-72, italics mine). This 'hypothesis' is not idle speculation, but what Burke would call 'a way of sizing up reality' in order to act within it (1974: 4), or as Goodman puts it, to 'cope with' a given 'experience' (1971: 171-2).

The importance of this suggestion lies in its link to a kind of 'critical realism' or even a 'promiscuous realism' (Graeber 2001: 52-53, Dupré 1981: 82): for Proudhon, 'nature, taken as a whole' can be seen to 'lend itself' to an indefinite variety of schemes of categorization (1927: 162, translation mine; May and Lance 1995: 980). Because 'there is no single way, even no normal way, of representing the world we experience,' because representation (and 'perception' and 'comprehension' *per se*) is 'a selection from chaos, a definition from the amorphous, a concretion within the "terrible fluidity" of life,' it has the power to help shape our experience, to redetermine how we interpret and respond to it (Read 1964: 21; Landauer 1974: 7-11, 78, translation mine; Read 1967: 31). In this sense, it matters greatly what 'hypothesis about how the world is' a text happens to embody. The 'representation of life' that it suggests to us, often independently of its explicit propositional content (and indeed, often largely independently of any conscious intention on the part of the author or authors), is highly political; 'every fiction prescribes as well as (or more than) it describes' – or prescribes *by* describing, acquires its performative force *through* its constativity. That is to say, a text embodies 'a worldview,' a 'view of what life 'really' is' – and, implicitly, of what it 'should be' (Wilson 1991: 54-55, 57).

11.

By 'life,' we mean not only the actual but the plural *potentials* which are dormant within it.

'Life,' here, is to be thought in fully natural, ecological terms, as 'a vast, complicated whole,' 'a world of becoming and transition in which multiple diversities coexist, a world of the never-completed, of the incalculable and the inextricable'; it is a process of '*uninterrupted creation*' (Voline 2005, 434-435; Landauer 1974: 77, translation mine). This living reality is conceived of as comprising both 'actuality,' that which is, and 'potentialities,' that which could be; the real cannot be reduced to either without falsification (Bookchin 1996: 21; Clark 1976: 27-28; McLaughlin 2002: 104-106; Graeber 2001, *Toward an Anthropological Theory* 52, 260). There is no potential which does not emerge from some concrete actuality; conversely, there is no actuality which does not harbour multiple potentialities, a 'multitude of modes of being and possibilities,' even if some of these possibilities are indeed 'monstrous' (Bookchin 1971: 284; Colson 2004: 12, Colson 2001: 246; Cochrane 2000: 168). To reduce history to a linear structure with a predetermined goal, in the manner of Comte, Hegel, or (at times) Marx and Engels, is to obscure the dimension of potentiality; on the other hand, to reduce history to a collection of infinitely interpretable, undecideable 'texts,' in the manner of Paul de Man, Jean Baudrillard, or (at times) Richard Rorty, is to overlook the dimension of actuality. Reality, from an anarchist perspective, is neither rigidly determined nor a shapeless void; it is a vast 'sum of transformations' which can neither be 'predetermined nor preconceived,' a 'field [which] is open before human spontaneity': 'the field of the possible' (Bakunin 1908: III.216; Proudhon 1935: III.407, translations mine; McLaughlin 2002: 104).

12.

Here, anarchist literary theory joins a larger anarchist critique of ideology: to the extent that we can speak of a 'false consciousness,' this falsehood consists in a.) the creation of relationships which are taken to be inescapably fixed (or, ontologically, the reduction of life's possibilities to the actually existing) or b.) the attempt to escape from all relationship (the reduction of life's reality to pure potentiality, unanchored to any actuality).

Anarchist analyses do not locate power, *potentia*, in a sovereign, nor do they reduce it to an epiphenomenon of economics; instead, they view it as 'immanent in society,' emerging from the matrix of relationships (Proudhon 1935: II.261, translation mine; Landauer quoted. in Lunn 1973: 226; Colson 2001: 31-33, translations mine). This 'social power' or 'collective force,' however, has been alienated from itself, so that it is consistently located *outside of the social* (Bakunin 1970: 43n; Proudhon 1935: II.269, translation mine; de Cleyre 2004: 69). This internment of power within a 'place of power' or displacement of power into a 'centre elsewhere' (God, human nature, the workings of the dialectic, etc.), itself a mystification of social life, is underwritten by other forms of false consciousness: certain conceptions of the world according to which 'freedom seems not only impossible ... but pernicious,' in a cycle of social reproduction, emerge to support the very 'social order' which 'has permitted and profited from' the circulation of these conceptions (Newman 2001:6; Derrida 1978: 279; Cunillera 1977: 289, translation mine). Among the many vehicles for the circulation of 'ideologies' – particularly in their claim to present a 'mirror of life' – are poetry, drama, and fiction (Birrell 1999:198; Baginski 1906: 36).

If reality, however ambiguous and 'promiscuous,' is not entirely formless and empty, if it has certain features that can be falsified, then any claim to imitate reality as it is, to hold up a 'mirror' to 'life,' must be regarded with suspicion; as Voline insists, 'we must discover and frame ... everything that ought to be regarded as phoney, at odds with life's reality and in need of rejection ... [and] everything that ought to be registered as just, wholesome, acceptable' (de Cleyre 1914: 361; Voline 2005: 435).

What is *a priori* 'false, fictitious, impossible and abstract', for anarchists, is what is taken to be 'fixed, complete, whole, inalterable' – in short, the 'Absolute' that Hegel stood at the end of his dialectic (Proudhon 1946: 50-51, translation mine). 'What we seek,' Proudhon writes, 'is a means of *purging the ideas* ... in other words, it is to eliminate the ABSOLUTE from the consideration of things' (1935: III.249, translation mine).

As Colson writes, we are in the presence of what can be called false consciousness when 'the "relative" is transformed into the "absolute," the "resultant" into an originating "principle," the effect into the cause, and the product of human activity into the dominatory foundation of this activity' (2004: 62). Thus, for instance, gold coin, as 'money,' the universal 'standard' of value, is taken to be the source of wealth: 'imagination attributing to the metal that which is the effect of collective thought manifested through the metal,' this object is fetishistically endowed with a power it does not have (Proudhon 1926: II.88-89, translation mine). Other forms of false consciousness entail obscuring one of the two aspects of the real – either collapsing the potential into the actual (reifying the status quo into an unchanging order or an inescapable necessity) or dispersing the actual into mere potentialities (the denial of every concrete limitation or determination in favour of an abstractly limitless possibility). Bakunin indicts the latter in his attack on theological idealism, which 'disdains all that exists' as mere finite particularity, seeking instead to found things in the 'complete negation' of the existing, i.e., God as 'the highest abstraction of the mind' or 'absolute nothingness'; he indicts the former in his critique of materialist determinism, which reduces 'the human point of view,' the standpoints of human subjects, to 'inevitable,' objective necessity, thereby eliminating the categories of the ethical 'should,' the 'ideal,' 'consciousness,' will, and desire (1972: 272, 309-313).

13.

This both implies and is implicated in an anarchist aesthetic which emerged most clearly in the late nineteenth century theory of *art social*, defined as the rejection both of Naturalism (which 'realistically' reifies life into actuality) and of Symbolism (which seeks to escape into an 'ideal' realm of potentiality), and as the affirmation of an art which would make visible the potentials within the actual, evoking the 'ideal' within the 'real.'

For Proudhon, since 'the ideal ... has its base, its cause, its power of development, in the real,' a genuinely realist art would have as its 'goal,' in fact, to evoke 'the *ideal*' (1935: III.585; 1939: 59, translation mine). Kropotkin identified 'this idea which so much shocked Western readers when Proudhon developed it' as a 'realism ... [with] an idealistic aim' (1916: 295, 86). From this perspective, realism cannot be 'reduced to a simple photography' of the actual; indeed, to do so would be to exclude the dimension of potentiality or 'the ideal' which is 'inherent in things,' and thereby to reify reality; likewise, to 'depart from the truth by way of the ideal,' in the manner of premodern art, was to shield the actual world from the critical gaze, superimposing an unchanging 'dogma' on the flux of appearances (Litvak 1988: 26-27; Lazare 1896: 29; Proudhon 1939: 61, 188, translations mine).

Elaborating on this conception a generation later, anarchists attacked both the Naturalist aesthetic of Émile Zola and Gerhard Hauptmann *and* the Symbolist aesthetic of Stéphane Mallarmé for their radical 'incompleteness': where the one, focusing our gaze on 'the lowest and most degenerate aspects' of the present reality, tends to issue in a resigned acceptance of the actual – 'tout comprendre, tout pardonner' – the other, seeking to escape the banality of everyday appearances, issues in a strikingly parallel affirmation of 'the old Romantic theory, the foundation of which is Christian: life is abject, one must go outside of life' (Granier 2003: II, 'Introduction''; Lunn 1973: 45; Lazare 1896: 27-28; Kropotkin, *Ideals* 86; Lunn 1973: 45; Lazare 1896: 28, translations mine).

Instead of a falsely polarized aesthetic realism or idealism, Proudhon argued, what was needed was an art which would combine 'observation' with 'inspiration,' revealing the possible within the actual (Litvak 1988: 26-27; Lazare 1896: 29; Proudhon 1939: 61, 188, 190-192, translations mine). Just as anarchists practice a prefigurative politics, they proposed to create 'a *prefigurative* art [*un art de précurseur*],' an art which would evoke the imagination of and a 'longing for' a better world (Lazare 1896: 31, translation and italics mine; Jacoby 2005: 85).

14.

Herein lies what could be called the *utopian* dimension of anarchist literary theory: not in the sense of positing an abstract ideal without relation to an actual *topos*, but in the sense that we are always journeying from one *topos* to another, travelling into the future.

Graeber proposes that an anarchist approach to the study of social texts might be modelled after a certain kind of 'auto-ethnography,' a practice of 'teasing out the tacit logic or principles underlying certain forms of radical practice, and then, not only offering the analysis back to those communities, but using them to formulate new visions ("if one applied the same principles as you are applying to political organization to economics, might it not look something like this?"...)': in other words, a 'utopian extrapolation' of the potential from the actual (2003). 'Utopia,' in Granier's words, 'thus becomes a *method*' (2003: II, 'Introduction,' translation and italics mine). It is in this sense that for anarchists, the act of interpretation is also a creative act (Dadoun 1997).

NOTES

1. See, for instance, Carol Vanderveer Hamilton's 'American Writers, Modernism, and Representations of the Sacco-Vanzetti Case' in this journal (vol. 8, no. 1, March 2000, pp. 3-25); H. Gustav Klaus's study of 'Silhouettes of Anarchism in the Work of Three British Writers' in Gisela Hermann-Brennecke and Wolf Kindermann, eds., *Anglo-American Awareness: Arpeggios in Aesthetics* (Münster, Germany: LIT, 2005, pp. 171-92); and the volume edited by Klaus with Stephen Knight, *'To Hell With Culture': Anarchism in Twentieth-Century British Literature* (Cardiff: University of Wales Press, 2005); or Arthur Efron's 'War is the Health of the State: An Anarchist Reading of *Henry IV, Part One*' (in *Works and Days* vol. 10, no. 1, Spring 1992 , pp. 7-75).

2. The dead end could be described as follows: embarrassed by the textualist excesses of the '80s, theorists have pursued a certain 'return to order' via a.) a textualized historical materialism, b.) a conversion of 'literary studies into cultural studies' (Easthope 1991), and c.) engagement in identity politics while gingerly seeking to avoid commitments to essentialism, totalizing narratives, and representation. Now we hear complaints from several quarters of a 'theory mess' (Rapaport 2001), reflecting a sense that in trying to have it both ways, accommodating relativism to realism and vice versa, the whole enterprise has become incoherent. The anarchist tradition, grounded in concrete ethico-political commitments and possessed of surprisingly powerful critical instruments, can point the way out of the maze.

WORKS CITED

Baginski, Max 1906. The Old and the New Drama. *Mother Earth* 1 (April): 36-42.

Bakunin, Michael 1908. Max Nettlau and James Guillaume, (eds.) *Oeuvres*. Paris, Stock.

—— 1970. *God and the State*. New York, Dover Books.

—— 1972. Sam Dolgoff, (ed. and trans.) *Bakunin on Anarchy: Selected Works by the Activist-Founder of World Anarchism*. New York, Alfred A. Knopf.

Barthes, Roland 1977. Stephen Heath, (ed. and trans.) *Image-Music-Text*. New York, Hill and Wang.

Birrell, Neil 1999. Notes on Culture and Ideology. *The Raven* 10 (39): 193-201.

Bookchin, Murray 1971. *Post-Scarcity Anarchism*. San Francisco, Ramparts Books.

—— 1996. *The Philosophy of Social Ecology: Essays on Dialectical Naturalism*. Montréal, Black Rose Books.

Burke, Kenneth 1974. *The Philosophy of Literary Form: Studies in Symbolic Action*. Berkeley, CA, University of California Press.

Castoriadis, Cornelius 1998. Karen Blamey, (trans.) *The Imaginary Institution of Society*. Cambridge, MA, MIT Press.

Clark, John P. 1976. *Max Stirner's Egoism*. London, Freedom Press.

Cochrane, Regina 2000. Left-Libertarian Ecopolitics and the Contradictions of

Naturalistic Ethics: The Teleology Issue in Social Ecology. *Democracy & Nature* 6 (July): 161-86.

Colombo, Eduardo 2002. À propos du *Petit Lexique philosophique de l'anarchisme de Daniel* Colson. *Réfractions* 8: 127-41.

Colson, Daniel 1998. Lectures anarchistes de Spinoza. *Réfractions* 2. <http://refractions.plusloin.org/textes/refractions2/spinoza-colson.html>

—— 2001. *Petit lexique philosophique de l'anarchisme de Proudhon à Deleuze.* Paris, Librairie générale française.

—— 2002. Réponse de Daniel Colson à Eduardo Colombo. *Réfractions* 8: 143-153.

—— 2004. *Trois essais de philosophie anarchiste: Islam, histoire, monadologie.* Paris, Léo Scheer.

Culler, Jonathan 1983. *On Deconstruction.* Ithaca, NY, Cornell University Press.

Cunillera, Angel 1977. ¿Que es el arte? In Equipo ERA 80, (ed.) *Els Anarquistes educadors del poble: 'La revista blanca' (1898-1905)* pp. 286-91.

Cunningham, Valentine 2002. *Reading After Theory.* Oxford, Blackwell.

Dadoun, Roger 1997. Pour une critique lit.-lib. *Réfractions* 1. <http://www.plusloin.org/refractions/textes/refractions1/DadounCritique.htm>

de Cleyre, Voltairine 1914. *Selected Works of Voltairine de Cleyre.* New York, Mother Earth Publishing Association.

—— 2004. A.J. Brigati, (ed.) *The Voltairine de Cleyre Reader.* Oakland, CA: AK Press.

Deleuze, Gilles and Félix Guattari 1987. Brian Massumi, (trans.) *A Thousand Plateaus.* Minneapolis, University of Minnesota Press.

Derrida, Jacques 1978. Gayatri Chakravorty Spivak, (trans.) *Writing and Difference.* Chicago, University of Chicago Press.

Dupré, John 1981. Natural Kinds and Biological Taxa. *Philosophical Review* 90: 66-90.

Easthope, Anthony 1991. *Literary Studies Into Cultural Studies.* London, Routledge.

Efron, Arthur 1992. War is the Health of the State: An Anarchist Reading of *Henry IV, Part One. Works and Days* 10.1: 7-75.

Ehrlich, Howard J. 1979. Notes and Queries of an Anarchist Critic. In Howard J. Ehrlich et al., (eds.) *Reinventing Anarchy: What Are Anarchists Thinking These Days?* pp. 361-364.

Faure, Sébastian (ed.) 1934. *Encyclopédie anarchiste.* Paris, Editions de la Librairie Internationale.

Fish, Stanley 1980. *Is There a Text in This Class? The Authority of Interpretive Communities.* Cambridge, MA, Harvard University Press.

Goodman, Paul 1964a. *Compulsory Mis-education and The Community of Scholars.* New York, Vintage Books.

—— 1964b. *Utopian Essays and Practical Proposals.* New York, Vintage Books.

—— 1971. *Speaking and Language: Defense of Poetry.* New York, Vintage Books.

Graeber, David 2001. *Toward an Anthropological Theory of Value: The False Coin of Our Own Dreams.* New York, Palgrave.

—— 2002. The New Anarchists. *New Left Review* 13: 61-73.

—— 2004a. *Fragments of an Anarchist Anthropology.* Chicago, Prickly Paradigm Press.

—— 2004b. The Twilight of Vanguardism. In Jai Sen, (ed.) *The World Social Forum: Challenging Empires* pp. 329-35.

Granier, Caroline 2003. *'Nous sommes des briseurs de formules': Les écrivains anarchistes en France à la fin du dix-neuvième siècle. Thèse de doctorat de l'Université Paris 8.* 17 July 2005. <http://raforum.apinc.org/rubrique.php3?id_rubrique=770>

Guérin, Daniel 1970. *Anarchism: From Theory to Practice.* New York, Monthly Review Press.

Hamilton, Carol Vanderveer 2000. American Writers, Modernism, and Representations of the Sacco-Vanzetti Case. *Anarchist Studies* 8.1: 3-25.

Jablon, Madelyn 1997. *Black Metafiction: Self-Consciousness in African-American Literature.* Iowa City, University of Iowa Press.

Jacoby, Russell 2005. *Picture Imperfect: Utopian Thought For An Anti-Utopian Age.* New York, Columbia University Press.

Jameson, Frederic 1972. *The Prison-House of Language: A Critical Account of Structuralism and Russian Formalism.* Princeton, NJ, Princeton University Press.

Klaus, H. Gustav. 'Silhouettes of Anarchism in the Work of Three British Writers.' In Gisela Hermann-Brennecke and Wolf Kindermann, (eds.), *Anglo-American Awareness: Arpeggios in Aesthetics.* Münster, Germany, LIT, 2005, pp. 171-92.

—— and Stephen Knight, (eds.), 2005. *'To Hell With Culture': Anarchism in Twentieth-Century British Literature.* Cardiff, University of Wales Press.

Kristeva, Julia 1986. Toril Moi, (ed.) *The Kristeva Reader.* New York, Columbia University Press.

Kropotkin, Peter 1916. *Ideals and Realities in Russian Literature.* New York, Alfred A. Knopf.

—— 1970. Roger N. Baldwin, (ed.) *Kropotkin's Revolutionary Pamphlets.* New York, Dover Books.

Landauer, Gustav 1974. *La Révolution.* Paris, Éditions Champ Libre.

Lazare, Bernard 1896. *L'Écrivain et l'art social.* Béarn, Bibliotheque de l'art social.

Leval, Gaston 2005. Libertarian Democracy. In Robert Graham, (ed.) *Anarchism: A Documentary History of Libertarian Ideas: Volume One: From Anarchy to Anarchism (300CE to 1939)* pp. 477-82.

Litvak, Lily 1988. *La mirada roja: estética y arte del anarquismo español, 1880-1913.* Barcelona, Ediciones del Serbal.

Lunn, Eugene D. 1973. *Prophet of Community: The Romantic Socialism of Gustav Landauer.* Berkeley, CA: University of California Press.

Lyotard, Jean-François 1984. Susan Hanson et al., (trans.) *Driftworks.* New York, Semiotext(e).

Magón, Ricardo Flores 1920. Carta del 30 de noviembre de 1920. Biblioteca Virtual Antorcha. <http://www.antorcha.net/biblioteca_virtual/politica/epis/carta_elena_30_noviembre_1920.html> 31 July 2006.

Malatesta, Errico 1993. Vernon Richards, (ed. and trans.) *Life and Ideas.* London, Freedom Press.

May, Todd, and Mark Lance 1995. Beyond Foundationalism and Its Opposites: Toward a Reasoned Ethics for Progressive Action. *American Behavioral Science* 38 (7): 976-89.

McLaughlin, Paul 2002. *Mikhail Bakunin: The Philosophical Basis of His Anarchism.* New York, Algora.

Newman, Saul 2001. *From Bakunin to Lacan: Anti-Authoritarianism and the Dislocation of Power.* Lanham, MD, Lexington.

Owens, Craig 1983. The Discourse of Others: Feminists and Postmodernism. In Hal Foster, (ed.) *The Anti-Aesthetic: Essays on Postmodern Culture* pp. 57-82.

Proudhon, Pierre-Joseph 1926. *Système des contradictions économiques, ou la philosophie de la misère.* Paris, Rivière.

—— 1927. *De la Création de l'ordre dans l'humanité.* Paris, Rivière.

—— 1935. *De la Justice dans la révolution et dans l'église.* Paris, Rivière.

—— 1936. *La Révolution sociale démontrée par le coup d'état du Deux-Décembre projet d'exposition perpétuelle.* Paris, Rivière.

—— 1939. *Du principe de d'art et de sa destination sociale.* Paris, Rivière.

—— 1946. *Philosophie du progrès.* Paris, Rivière.

Rapaport, Herman 2001. *The Theory Mess: Deconstruction in Eclipse.* New York, Columbia University Press.

Read, Herbert 1938. *Poetry and Anarchism.* London, Faber & Faber.

—— 1964. *The Philosophy of Modern Art: Collected Essays.* London, Faber and Faber.

—— 1967. *Poetry and Experience.* New York, Horizon Press.

Rorty, Richard 1982. *Consequences of Pragmatism: Essays, 1972-1980.* Minneapolis, University of Minnesota Press.

Shapiro, Michael J. 1992. *Reading the Postmodern Polity: Political Theory as Textual Practice.* Minneapolis, Minnesota University Press.

Spanos, William V. 1979. Heidegger, Kierkegaard, and the Hermeneutic Circle: Towards a Postmodern Theory of Interpretation as Dis-closure. In William V. Spanos, (ed.) *Martin Heidegger and the Question of Literature: Towards a Postmodern Literary Hermeneutics* pp. 115-148.

Vaneigem, Raoul 1994. Donald Nicholson-Smith, (trans.) *The Revolution of Everyday Life.* Seattle, WA, Left Bank Books.

Voline 2005. Anarchist Synthesis. In Robert Graham, (ed.) *Anarchism: A Documentary History of Libertarian Ideas: Volume One: From Anarchy to Anarchism (300CE to 1939)* pp. 431-435.

Wilson, Peter Lamborn 1991. Amoral Responsibility. *Science Fiction EYE* 8: 54-57.

Deleuze, Derrida, and anarchism

N. J. JUN

Department of Philosophy
Purdue University
100 North University Street
West Lafayette, Indiana 47907
njun@purdue.edu

ABSTRACT

In this paper, I argue that Deleuze's political writings and Derrida's early (pre-1985) work on deconstruction affirms the tactical orientation which Todd May in particular has associated with 'poststructuralist anarchism.' Deconstructive philosophy, no less than Deleuzean philosophy, seeks to avoid closure, entrapment, and structure; it seeks to open up rather than foreclose possibilities, to liberate rather than interrupt the flows and move-ments which produce life. To this extent, it is rightfully called an anarchism – not the utopian anarchism of the nineteenth century, perhaps, but the provisional and preconditional anarchism which is, and will continue to be, the foundation of postmodern politics.

I.

From Proudhon to the Paris commune, anarchist movements occupied an important place in the history of French radical politics until the end of the Second World War, when they were driven to near extinction by the triumph of the Soviet-backed French Communist Party (PCF).[1] This situ-ation had begun to change dramatically by the early 1960s, however, owing to the increasing influence of so-called 'New Left' theory, the rise of the youth movement, and growing antagonism on the left toward Soviet-sponsored terrorism. For the first time in a long time, leftist intellectuals were no longer content to make apologies for Marxist-Leninist orthodoxy and were instead seeking viable alternatives to it.

The visible culmination of this process was, of course, the uprisings of May 1968 in France, which marked the first significant revolutionary event in the twentieth century that was carried out not only independently of the Communist Party, but in flagrant opposition to it as well. Unlike the fundamentally vanguardist revolutions of Russia, China, Vietnam and Cuba, the Paris Spring was fomented in mostly spontaneous fashion by a decentralized and non-hierarchical confederation of students and workers who harboured a common scepticism toward grand political narratives. At the forefront of this confederation were the *Enragés*, a group of revolutionaries who sought to reinvent anarchist theory and practice.[2]

Unlike the FAI/CNT during the Spanish Civil War, the *Enragés* were not so much an organized faction as a loose collection of individuals representing a variety of political persuasions. They were not anarchists in the narrow ideological sense of belonging to a particular anarchist movement or endorsing a particular theory of anarchism (e.g., anarcho-syndicalism).[3] On the contrary, the *Enragés* had little to do with the French Anarchist Federation,[4] nor with any other residua of the pre-1945 European anarchist movement.[5] While some, like Daniel Cohn-Bendit, were indeed associated with organizations more closely related to traditional anarchism, several belonged to Marxist-oriented groups such as the Situationist International, *Socialisme ou Barbarie*, and *Informations Correspondance Ouvrieres*.[6] As Cohn-Bendit stated of his comrades, 'Some read Marx, of course, perhaps Bakunin, and of the moderns, Althusser, Mao, Guevara, Lefebvre. Nearly all the militants of the movement have read Sartre.'[7] Other influences included:

> Trotskyist criticism of Soviet society … Mao Tse-tung on the question of the revolutionary alliance with the peasant masses, and Marcuse when it comes to demonstrating the repressive nature of modern society or when the latter proclaims that everything must be destroyed in order that everything could be rebuilt.[8]

Classical anarchist theories and movements, as such, were only one source of inspiration among many, and as with all such sources, the *Enragés* did not regard them as infallible.[9]

The *Enragés* were anarchists in the more important and fundamental sense of advocating certain principles, such as opposition to centralization, hierarchy, and repressive power, that are common to all forms of anarchism.[10] It is precisely the realization of such principles in practice, however, that made May 1968 such a decisive turning point in the history of radical politics.[11] For example, despite the enormous influence they enjoyed throughout the uprisings, the *Enragés* refused to betray their anti-authoritarian beliefs by taking on leadership roles of any sort.[12] Moreover, they repeatedly thwarted attempts by others to consolidate the leadership of the movement, thereby preventing its appropriation by outside political parties.[13] Ultimately, centralized leadership was replaced with democratic, self-managing councils such as the Sorbonne Student Soviet and the Commune of Nantes.[14] As a result, the anarchist-controlled universities 'became cities unto themselves, with virtually everything necessary for normal life.'[15]

Although such successes were short-lived, the uprisings having been quelled after only six weeks, the events of May 1968 had far-reaching and lasting effects. Among other things, they marked the end of the Stalinist

PCF's longstanding dominance over the French Left,[16] laid the foundation for the German and Italian *Autonomia* movements of the 1970s and 1980s, and would eventually exert a profound influence on various anti-globalization movements of the 1990s. They also radicalized a whole new generation of intellectuals including the subjects of the present inquiry, Gilles Deleuze and Jacques Derrida.

Unlike his long-time friend and collaborator Felix Guattari, who had been involved in radical activism since the early 1960s, Deleuze did not become politically active until after 1968.[17] 'From this period onward,' writes Paul Patton, 'he became involved with a variety of groups and causes, including the *Groupe d'Information sur les Prisons* (GIP) begun by Foucault and others in 1972.'[18] More importantly, Deleuze's prior commitment to speculative metaphysics gave way to a deep interest in political philosophy as he attempted to make sense of the political practices he encountered in 1968. Four years later, in 1972, Deleuze and Guattari published *Anti-Oedipus: Capitalism and Schizophrenia*, the first of a two-volume work on political philosophy.[19] The second volume, entitled *A Thousand Plateaus*, followed eight years later.[20]

From the 1960s until shortly before his death, Derrida, too, was a committed political activist, and this despite having had certain misgivings with the events of 1968. During the 1980s, for example, he campaigned tirelessly against everything from apartheid to the death penalty. At the same time, however, it was not until the mid-1990s that Derrida began to write about explicitly ethical and political topics.[21] This has led various writers to conclude that deconstruction as such is inherently apolitical, or else that it is useless as a radical political praxis.[22]

We shall return to this point below. In the meantime, it is worth noting that, not long after the appearance of Deleuze and Guattari's *Anti-Oedipus*, Gayatry Spivak and Michael Ryan published a groundbreaking analysis of the connections between poststructuralist philosophy (including that of Derrida, Deleuze, and Guattari) and the *nouvel anarchisme* of 1968.[23] This was followed throughout the next twenty-seven years by a series of books and articles arguing that poststructuralist political philosophy represented a new kind of anarchism[24] variously referred to as 'postanarchism,'[25] 'postmodern anarchism,'[26] and 'poststructuralist anarchism.'[27]

Todd May in particular has argued at great length for an anarchist reading of Deleuze – one which, to my mind at least, is highly successful. At the same time, however, May makes a crucial mistake in trying to found Deleuzean anarchism upon *normativity*, a concept which Deleuze, like Nietzsche and Spinoza before him, repeatedly rejects. As I shall argue in parts three and four of this paper, the salient difference between classical anarchism and Deleuzean anarchism is that the latter involves a turn away from the normative and a concomitant movement toward the *ethical*. *Pace*

May, it is precisely this turn which gives Deleuze's political philosophy a decisive advantage over that of his forebears.

May and his confreres have been oddly silent about Derrida. This is not to say that nothing has been written about Derrida's politics, but (a) most of this writing focuses on Derrida's later 'political turn' and (b) with few exceptions,[28] none of it frames the analysis in terms of *anarchism*. In part five of this paper, I shall address the oft-overlooked political ramifications of Derrida's earlier and more important works on deconstruction. I will argue, moreover, that deconstruction provides a framework for anarchism that is different from, but harmonious with, Deleuzean anarchism.

II.

The primary focus of Deleuze's early works is metaphysics and the history of philosophy. Though they can hardly be called 'apolitical,' the political dimension of books like *Difference and Repetition* (1968) tends to be so vague and understated as to require extraction by skilled exegetes. This is not true of the two volumes of *Capitalism and Schizophrenia*, the political emphasis of which is made quite explicit at the outset. Like all of Deleuze's works, however, *C & S* is so formidably dense and complicated that we cannot begin to do it justice in an essay of this size. Instead we will limit ourselves to a brief 'thematic overview' of those ideas and concepts which illustrate the *anarchistic* dimension of Deleuze's political thought, taking care to note their similarities with and differences from related ideas and concepts in classical anarchism.

Anarchism places an enormous emphasis on power or, more specifically, on what could be referred to as 'coercive' or 'repressive power.' Although Deleuze does discuss power, especially in his book on Foucault,[29] he is generally more inclined to speak in terms of *forces* – e.g., active vs. reactive forces in his book on Nietzsche,[30] forces of desire vs. social forces in *Anti-Oedipus*, etc. (For purposes of this essay, we will regard 'force' as more or less synonymous with 'power,' at least in the Foucauldian sense.[31]) Our initial question, therefore, is what force is and how it operates according to Deleuze.

In one decidedly aphoristic passage, Deleuze claims there are only forces of desire and social forces.[32] Although Deleuze tends to regard desire as a creative force (in the sense that it produces rather than represses its object) and the social as a force which 'dams up, channels, and regulates' the flow of desire,[33] he does not mean to suggest that there are two distinct *kinds* of forces which differentially affect objects exterior to themselves. On the contrary, there is only a single, unitary force which manifests itself in particular 'assemblages.'[34] Each of these assemblages, in turn, contains within itself both desire and various 'bureaucratic or fascist pieces' which seek to subjugate and annihilate that desire.[35] Neither force acts or works upon pre-existent objects; rather everything that exists is alternately created and/or destroyed in accordance with the particular assemblage which gives rise to it.

As May notes by way of summary, 'power does not suppress desire; rather it is implicated in every assemblage of desire.'[36] Existing things are constituted ('assembled') by forces that are immanent to them; 'concrete social fields' are therefore affects of complex movements and connections of forces which vary in intensity over time.[37] For Deleuze, forces are principally distinguished according to their affects, which in turn are distinguished according to whether they are *life-affirming* or *life-denying* at the level of *life itself*.[38] Unlike the concept of 'coercive power,' which has a kind of built-in normativity, the concepts of life-affirming/denying are, in the first instance at least, *purely descriptive*; that is, they describe the way forces produce reality and nothing else.

Given the ubiquitous and ontologically constitutive nature of force, it goes without saying that force *simpliciter* cannot be 'abolished' or even 'resisted.' As we shall see, this does not mean that *repressive* social forces cannot be opposed. It does imply, however, that for Deleuze (as for Spinoza), the question is not whether and how resistance is possible, but rather how and why desire comes to repress and ultimately destroy itself in the first place.[39] This requires, among other things, an analysis of the various assemblages that come into being over time (*vis a vis* their affects) as well as the experimental pursuit of alternative assemblages at the level of praxis.

According to Deleuze, repressive forces do not emanate from a unitary source but rather within multiple sites. The complex interconnection of these sites, moreover, is precisely what gives rise to the social world (this is what he means when he suggests that power is 'rhizomatic' as opposed to 'arboreal').This is not to say that power does not become concentrated within certain sites; indeed, much of *Capitalism and Schizophrenia* is given over to an analysis of such concentrations as they manifest themselves in particular political and economic forms. What this analysis reveals is a constant conflict between (for example) the State-form, which seeks to 'overcode' and 'territorialize' desire, and various modes of desire itself, which seek to 'reterritorialize' themselves along 'lines of flight.' Similar analyses could no doubt be afforded of the 'Church-form,' the 'gender-form,' and countless other sites of concentrated power. In all such cases, however, one and the same force is simultaneously seeking to escape and re-conquer itself, and it is precisely this tension which allows ostensibly 'revolutionary' or 'liberatory' movements (e.g., Bolshevism) to occasionally metamorphose into totalitarian regimes (e.g., Stalinist Russia).

To a certain important extent, classical anarchism shares Deleuze's emphasis on the multifarious and rhizomatic nature of power.[40] Unlike Marxism and other 'strategic' political philosophies which identify a unitary locus of repressive power, the 'tactical' political philosophies of Deleuze and his anarchist predecessors 'perform [their] analyses within a milieu characterized ... by the tension between irreducible and mutually intersecting practices of power.'[41] As David Wieck notes, '[classical] anarchism is more than anti-statism, even if government (the state) is, appropriately, the central focus of anarchist critique.'[42] As 'the generic social and political idea that expresses negation of all [repressive] power'[43] anarchism rejects all forms of coercive authority, including, but not limited to, the 'sombre trinity' – state, capital and the church.[44] This analysis was later extended by thinkers like Deleuze, Foucault and Derrida to power relations at the level of discursive practices (e.g., the production of theories of truth and knowledge) as well as economies of desire.

This is what leads May to conclude – rightly, I think – that there is a strong affinity between classical anarchism and Deleuzean philosophy. At the same time, however, much of *The Political Philosophy of Poststructuralist Anarchism* is devoted to showing that there are irreconcilable differences between the two. For example, he alleges that classical anarchism depends upon an essentialistic conception of human nature which Deleuze and other poststructuralists have systematically dismantled.[45] Likewise, he insists that the classical anarchists regard *all* power as repressive even though they also acknowledge that power emerges from multiple sources.[46] As we have just seen, this is exactly what Deleuze's analysis of power seeks to disprove.

I shall not speak to the first charge concerning human nature, as this has already been addressed masterfully by my colleague Jesse Cohn.[47] Instead I will briefly respond to the second charge before turning to what I see as the *crucial* difference between classical anarchism and Deleuzean anarchism – viz., the former's reliance on normativity. According to May, 'Power constitutes for the anarchists a suppressive force. The image of power with which anarchism operates is that of a weight pressing down – and at times destroying – the actions, events, and desires with which it comes in contact.'[48] In fact, power for the classical anarchists (as for many of the classical liberals) is in fact neither 'productive' nor 'repressive' *in and of itself*. Put another way, it is not as though there are two *types* of power – one 'productive' and one 'repressive' – which exist alongside and compete with one another.

On the contrary, manifestations of power are distinguished according to their *effects*. These effects, in turn, are distinguished according to their relative *justifiability* within a universalizable normative scheme that is both prior and exterior to power itself. Repressive power is only a species of 'power to,' which is at least analogous if not identical to Deleuze's all-encompassing 'force.' The only real difference is that 'repressive power' in the classical paradigm involves the forcible or even violent compulsion of bodies (what Foucault calls 'biopower') whereas repressive forces in the Deleuze scheme principally work to subjugate *desires*.[49] Here the classical anarchists' oversight has more to do with being historically antecedent to the powerful forces of mass media and state-controlled propaganda outlets than with simple ignorance. To this extent, May's insistence that all power is repressive for the classical anarchists and that *this* is an important way to distinguish them from Deleuze is quite misguided.

Equally misguided is May's attempt to found Deleuzean anarchism on a pair of normative principles which, though intimated below the surface of Deleuze's writings, are nonetheless mere variations on the 'principle of anti-authoritarianism' in classical anarchism (i.e., the principle that oppressive power ought to be opposed). Although he is correct to point out that Deleuze 'promotes' ways of thinking and acting that affirm life, this promotion need not – indeed, cannot – be cashed out in terms of normativity. In the next and last section, we will explore May's argument in a bit more detail and try to identify exactly where it goes wrong. In so doing, we will present an alternative reading of Deleuzean anarchism which provides a much better illustration of its differences with classical anarchism.

III.

In the final chapter of *The Political Philosophy of Poststructuralist Anarchism*, May rehearses the oft-repeated accusation that poststructuralism engenders a kind of moral nihilism.[50] Such an accusation is a product, May thinks, of the poststructuralists' general unwillingness to 'refer existence to transcendent values,' which if nothing else is the dominant strategy of much traditional moral philosophy in the West.[51] Strangely, May goes to great and eminently accurate lengths to explain why Deleuze rejects classical 'ethics,' only to argue that certain of Deleuze's other commitments implicitly contradict this rejection. As he notes:

> [Deleuze] praises Spinoza's *Ethics*, for instance, because it 'replaces Morality ...' For Deleuze, as for Nietzsche, the project of measuring life against external standards constitutes a betrayal rather than an affirmation of life. Alternatively, an ethics of the kind Spinoza has offered ... seeks out the possibilities life offers rather than denigrating life by appeal to 'transcendent values.' Casting the matter in more purely Nietzschean terms, the project of evaluating a life by reference to external standards is one of allowing reactive forces to dominate active ones, where reactive forces are those which 'separate active force from what it can do.[52]

In the same breath, however, May argues that Deleuze provides no explicit means by which to distinguish active forces from reactive ones beyond a vague appeal to 'experimentation.'[53] Such a means, he thinks, can only be discovered by extracting 'several intertwined and not very controversial ethical principles' from the hidden nooks of the Deleuzean corpus.

The first such principle, which May terms the 'antirepresentationalist principle,' is that 'practices of representing others to themselves – either in who they are or in what they want – ought, as much as possible to be avoided.'[54] The second, which he calls the 'principle of difference,' holds that 'alternative practices, all things being equal, ought to be allowed to flourish and even to be promoted.'[55] In both cases, May provides ample textual evidence to demonstrate that Deleuze (*inter alia*) is implicitly committed to the values underlying these principles. I think his analysis in this regard is very astute, as it is very clear from the foregoing that (for example) 'Gilles Deleuze's commitment to promoting different ways of thinking and acting is a central aspect of his thought.'[56] What I take issue with is the idea that the avowal of such values, implicit or otherwise, is *a fortiori* an avowal of specific normative principles.

As May himself notes, the defining characteristics of normativity are precisely abstraction, universality, and exteriority to life, all of which Deleuze seeks to undermine in his analysis of power. Although he argues that Deleuze's unwillingness to prescribe universalizable norms is itself motivated by a commitment to the aforesaid principles, this amounts to claiming that Deleuze is self-referentially inconsistent; it does not lead, as May thinks, to a general absolution of the charge of moral nihilism. If it is true that Deleuze scorns representation and affirms difference – and I think it is – the operative values cannot be articulated and justified by means of representation or the suppression of difference except on pain of dire contradiction. This is precisely the opposite of what May wishes to argue.

May is correct to point out that classical anarchism relies on a normative principle, as we noted briefly in the previous section. But it is precisely through its radical rejection of normativity that Deleuze's anarchism is to be distinguished. Rather than attempt to refine the principle of antiauthoritarianism so as to make it conform with the commonplaces of post-Kantian moral philosophy, May should instead recognize and celebrate the radical alternative that is being proposed. That alternative, as he himself points out, is precisely a turn to *ethics* in the Spinozistic sense of the term. It is the ethical, after all, which underlies the Deleuzian concept of experimentation as well as related concepts like Foucault's 'care of the self.' The question, of course, is what such an ethics would entail.

We already know that ethics is to be distinguished from morality on the basis of its concreteness, particularity, and interiority to life itself. Rather than posing universal codes of conduct grounded in abstract concepts like 'rationality,' ethics is instead concerned with the myriad ways in which lives can be led. To this extent, the traditional notion that ethics is concerned with *values* rather than *norms* is not entirely unfitting. Clearly values can be and often are universalized and rendered transcendent, as in the case of natural law theory. Even the Greeks, for whom value was a function of particular standards of excellence proper to particular things, believed that such standards were uniform for all human beings. One of Deleuze's great insights, however, is that every human being is the product of a unique and complicated multiplicity of forces, which means – among other things – that there are as many 'standards of excellence' as there are human persons. The value of 'difference' and disvalue of 'representation' are simply consequences of this fact; only *I* can discover, through the process of experimentation, what it means for me to be excellent – that is, what things are valuable in my life, what I ought to pursue and avoid, etc. Only through the process of pursuing alternative practices can I begin to discover the manifold possibility of value.

Deleuze's explicit rejection of the idea that there is any sort of 'natural' hierarchy of values among individuals is what grounds – indeed, necessitates – his anarchism. As he notes time and again in *Capitalism and Schizophrenia*, the authority of oppressive assemblages is always justified by assuming that certain peoples' values are, in some sense, *weightier* than those of others, and it is precisely the function of normativity to conceal the arbitrary and artifical nature of this assumption under the guise of universalizability and transcendence.

The process of creating value therefore requires an *eternal* revolution against the forces of repression wherever and however they arise. It lacks any kind of *telos* or end goal, since there is always a microfascism lurking at the heart of every system of personal value-construction which can, and often will, reterritorialize and overcode that system. Again, such a microfascism is every bit as instrumental in producing value as, say, the desire for freedom. It is not the case, therefore, that we *ought* to oppose authority, but rather that we *must* if we are to ever achieve value at all. The fact that the discovery of value is always provisional, tentative, and contingent is hardly a reason not to pursue it. In the end, there may be no ultimate means by which to distinguish one way of living from another, but it is precisely our inability to secure such a means which necessitates the perpetual pursuit of 'anarchy.'

IV.

Thus far I have provided a brief overview of the political and intellectual milieu within which Deleuze's and Derrida's thought evolved. I then provided an analysis of Deleuze's own incredibly novel reconstruction of anarchist philosophy. For Deleuze – and, to a certain extent, the classical anarchists – power is both ubiquitous and constitutive. Both deny that power is *either* productive *or* repressive, focusing instead on power's complex vacillations between these two poles, and they argue that power emanates from multiple sites. The true difference between them, as I have argued, concerns not the operation of power but rather the nature and justification of resistance. For the classical anarchists, this justification ultimately and ironically resides in an authoritarian structure – viz., normativity. For Deleuze, in contrast, it resides in the complete and total rejection of abstraction and the affirmation of personalized, particularized discoveries of value. It is precisely this emphasis on the ethical which renders Deleuzian anarchism both distinct from and superior to that of its forebears.

Derrida, as we intimated earlier, is in some sense a more difficult case. Bertrand Russell once noted that Spinoza, despite being 'the noblest and most lovable of the great philosophers,' was nonetheless viewed as a 'man of appalling wickedness during his lifetime and for a century after his death.'[57] One could make a similar claim about Derrida who, though universally regarded as one of the most prolific and influential philosophers of our time, is also one of the most controversial. Revered by some and despised by others, Derrida is simultaneously visionary and reactive, profound and sophistical, intrepid and nihilistic.[58] Such a reputation is doubly complicated given the widespread tendency on both sides to completely misunderstand Derrida and/or manipulate him for their own ends. Consider, for example, the scores of anti-Derrida polemics that were produced throughout the 1980s and 90s by everyone from literary/critical theorists[59] to analytic philosophers[60] to conservative cultural warriors.[61]

Of particular relevance to the present essay are those polemics which specifically accuse deconstruction of being apolitical,[62] counterrevolutionary,[63] or simply useless as a political praxis.[64] Though I am hardly alone in suggesting that such polemics are misguided,[65] few who would defend the radical implications of deconstruction have framed their defence in terms of anarchism.[66] As I shall argue, Derrida's inability or unwillingness to 'reconcile' deconstruction with Marxism is not the result of a philosophical failure[67] so much as a successful rejection of strategic political philosophy. Far from being a concession to the status quo, this rejection instead places deconstruction within the diverse family of theories broadly known as 'post-Marxist' and, with increasing frequency, 'poststructuralist anarchist.'

The aforesaid polemics are typically directed against certain ideas and concepts which, when taken together, form the basis of deconstructive theory. Although the 'meanings' of said ideas/concepts remain fundamentally consistent throughout the entire Derridean corpus, Derrida nonetheless adopts a variety of different terms to describe them. (For example, the 'foundational' Derridean concept of the transcendental signified is variously described as 'logocentrism,' 'phallogocentrism,' and 'the metaphysics of presence.' The same is true of other concepts such as trace, metaphoricity, the supplement, and so on.) As an exhaustive discussion of all such terms would take us well beyond the scope of this paper, we will instead focus our attention on the basic concepts underlying them – specifically those concepts that are most crucial to understanding Derrida's project.

One such concept is undecidability – that is, the impossibility, within language, of achieving any sort of fixed/static/transcendent meaning. Derrida articulates this concept in part through a critique of Saussurian linguistics. Broadly construed, Saussure's theory involves the differentiation of words (phonetic sounds which signify concepts), concepts (ideas which are signified by words), and referents (objects in the 'real world' which are signified by both ideas and words).[68] Saussure is frequently regarded as the first thinker to affirm the arbitrary relationship between words and the concepts they represent,[69] but his true accomplishment is the discovery that words actually derive their meaning from their differential relationships to other words, rather than correspondence to an arbitrary concept.[70] Derrida goes a step further by arguing that there are no concepts behind the signifiers – in other words, that the notion of a 'transcendent signifier' existing outside the play of linguistic differences is illusory.

Midway through his essay *Differance*, Derrida uses Saussure to develop a distinction between the absent and the present: 'We ordinarily say that a sign is put in place of the thing itself, the present thing – 'thing' holding here for the sense as well as the referent. Signs represent the present in its absence; they take the place of the present.'[71] Thus the sign is a kind of intermediary between the sensible and the intelligible; we think we are aware of presence even though it is absent to perception *vis-a-vis* the sign. The problem, Derrida says, is that 'the sign is conceivable only on the basis of the presence that it defers and in view of the deferred presence one intends to reappropriate.'[72] Because we cannot perceive presence except through the mediation of signs, presence can no longer be regarded as 'the absolutely matrical form of being'; rather, it becomes merely an effect of language.[73]

A word, therefore, never corresponds to a presence and so is always 'playing' off other words.[74] And because all words are necessarily trapped within this state of play (which Derrida terms '*difference*'), language as a whole cannot have a fixed, static, determinate – in a word, *transcendent* meaning; rather, *differance* 'extends the domain and the play of signification infinitely.'[75] Furthermore, if it is impossible for presence to have meaning apart from language, and if (linguistic) meaning is always in a state of play, it follows that presence itself will be indeterminate – which is, of course, precisely what it *cannot* be.[76] Without an 'absolute matrical form of being,' meaning becomes dislodged, fragmented, groundless, and elusive.

One immediate consequence of this critique is a disruption of the binary logic upon which much of Western thought is based. There are many reasons for this, but one is that binary logic derives difference from absolute metaphysical identity (read: presence) and not the other way around. (i.e., the law of identity: A = A, not just A = ~B, ~C, ~D ...; and the law of non-contradiction: A cannot be ~A at the same time and in the same respect). As we have just seen, however, nothing is what it is independently of the play of differences; there is no signified that transcends its relationship to the 'differential network' of signifiers.

Derrida articulates and expands upon this general criticism of the 'metaphysics of presence' in various texts and applies it to a wide range of binary concepts. In *Of Grammatology*, for example, he attacks the idea that writing is a 'supplement' to speech in the sense that the former (which is marked by absence) 'stands in' for the latter (which is marked by presence).[77] Elsewhere he discusses truth and falsity,[78] logic and illogic,[79] etc. All such discussions attempt to unearth *aporias* (i.e., impassable logical contradictions) within binary structures with a mind to undermining the logico-metaphysical groundwork upon which they are founded.

In the place of this groundwork Derrida offers a different model which he calls the 'logic of supplementarity.' As M.J. Devaney points out:

> This 'other' logic has been repressed and excluded by the history of philosophy. Whereas binary logic operates within the limits of an exclusive disjunction ('either ... or ...'), Derrida's undecidable logic of supplementarity is a logic of 'both ... and ...' that resists and disorganizes classical binary thinking.[80]

While binary logic is constructed on fundamental axioms such as the law of identity (A=A) and the law of noncontradiction (~[A ? ~A]), 'undecidable' logic is derived from the conjunction both A and not-A.[81] Derrida provides many examples of this logic, most notably the *pharmakon* – a substance which is both a poison and a remedy (hence something that is both A and ~A simultaneously).[82] Because the *pharmakon* is both A and ~A, he says, it does not have any *absolute* identity or *essential* meaning; therefore, binary logic does not apply to it.[83] (I will say more about this below.)

Given this deconstructive framework, what political implications, if any, can we draw from it? Here we ought first to consider some of Derrida's own words. In his early essay 'Structure, Sign and Play,' Derrida articulates a decidedly tactical position, one which spurns all longing for presence (read: unitary sources of oppression as well as predetermined liberartory *teloi* and utopias) and urges the deconstructive radical to 'play the game without security' and to affirm 'a world of signs' that 'determines the non-center otherwise than as the loss of center.'[84] In 'Différance,' moreover, he argues that:

> In the delineation of deconstruction everything is strategic and adventurous. Strategic because no transcendent truth present outside the field of writing can govern theologically the totality of the field. Adventurous because this strategy is not a simple strategy in the sense that strategy orients tactics according to a final goal, a *telos* or theme of domination, a mastery and ultimate reappropriation of the field.[85]

The 'adversary' of deconstruction, against which it wages its strategic and adventurous battle, is not a unitary source of oppressive power but rather the multiplicity of totalized binary oppositions which are constantly and variously manifesting themselves within multiple sites of oppression.[86] It does so, moreover, by 'overturning,' 'displacing,' 'resisting,' 'disorganizing,' and 'transgressing' these oppositions wherever they arise.[87]

Like Foucault, for whom power is always and only known through its affects, or Deleuze, for whom bodies without organs are always and only known through the desiring machines which attach to them, Derrida insists that binary oppositions are always and only known through their manifestations as relations of power. They are not, in other words, merely linguistic phenomena that can be known and analyzed independently of the political strategies and institutions within which they are encoded. As Barbara Foley notes:

> A political act of exclusion or subordination masks itself as a feature neutrally present in language (and representation) itself. Deconstruction seeks to counter this hegemony not by 'constituting a third term' or 'abolishing' the opposition, but by exposing its internal contradictions.[88]

To do otherwise, Derrida thinks, is to risk 'resurrecting' the very oppressive structure which radical political praxis seeks to destroy, as such techniques merely substitute one authority for another.[89] For Derrida, tactical political praxis is instead a 'technique of trouble'[90] whose only goal is to 'undermine the epistemological grounds upon which any authority presumes to rest.'[91]

Along with Foucault and Deleuze, Derrida insists that the principal vehicles through which binary opposition is manifested in multiple sites of oppressive power are representation and the suppression of difference. The two are related, as we have seen, because any act of representation is by definition an attempt to fix the identity of the other, to relegate it to the same. For Derrida, however, representation specifically involves the imposition of structures upon the play of differences – structures which involve both naming and logical deductions founded upon naming.[92] This process inevitably involves privileging certain referents ('names') as originary, as the very sources or foundations of thought, identifying them as the 'absolutely central form[s] of Being' and presuming them to be transparently 'present' to and constitutive of language.[93] What deconstruction demonstrates is that the act of representation is always and already generated through a prior (and ultimately foundationless) process of textualization which is always and already political. Thus 'presence' is merely a '[political] determination and … an effect.'[94]

Logocentrism, which for Derrida is the reactionary 'ideology' *par excellence*, is marked not just by its *complicity* with oppressive power relations but the role it plays in *producing* them. Derrida is careful to note, however, that even 'revolutionary discourses' can be and often are logocentric insofar as they represent themselves via problematic binary oppositions – e.g., bourgeois versus proletariat, oppression versus liberation, etc. Moreover, whereas such discourses tend to operate by way of reacting against (and, by extension, negating) whatever binary component they seek to oppose, deconstruction proceeds instead by way of '*différance*,' calling attention to the unstable, aporetic nature of all binary structures rather than defining itself against oppressive structures. This makes sense, after all, since all structures are in some sense oppressive, or at least capable of generating oppression when they become fixed, static, and totalized.

As we noted earlier, many have argued that Derrida's work prior to *Spectres of Marx* lacks any specific political content or else mystifies political discourse by avoiding concrete political situations. Although the examples we have looked at thus far are indeed fairly abstract, this is not true across the board. In 'The Ends of Man' (written during the Paris Spring), for example, Derrida attempts to analyze the West's imperialistic 'ethnological, economic, political, [and] military relationship' to the so-called Third World in terms of the strategy of binary opposition. On his view, anti-imperialism can only emerge 'on the ground' *within* the oppressed Third World; the task of radicals *outside* the Third World, in contrast, is 'to engage in the dual deconstructive activity of overturning and transgressing.'[95] Elsewhere in 'The White Mythology' he notes:

Metaphysics – the white mythology which reassembles and reflects the culture of the West: the white man takes his own mythology, Indo-European mythology, his own logos, that is, the *mythos* of his idiom, for the universal form of thought he must still wish to call Reason ... White mythology-metaphysics has erased within itself the fabulous scene that has produced it, the scene that nevertheless remains active and stirring, inscribed in white ink, an invisible design covered over in the palimpsest.[96]

Here Derrida shows how metaphysics (and the underlying mechanisms of metaphysics, e.g. 'reason') operates beneath the surface as an ideological justification for racism and colonialism. One cannot help but detect a passionate opposition here to the forces which metaphysics seeks to mystify and conceal. (This is hardly surprising given Derrida's own status as a French Algerian Jew.)

Similar examples from Derrida's pre-1994 *oeuvre* could no doubt be afforded,[97] but for our purposes it is sufficient to note that for Derrida deconstruction has never been a mere academic enterprise divorced from concrete political situations. On the contrary, as Barbara Foley notes, it is 'an epistemological practice possessing the capacity to expose and disrupt the ideological stratagems by which advanced capitalist society legitimates itself.'[98] Not surprisingly, Derrida has often attacked certain American students of deconstruction – most notably the members of the so-called 'Yale School' – who have attempted (whether consciously or unconsciously, explicitly or implicitly) to divest deconstruction of its radical political implications.[99] For Derrida, again, deconstruction operates as a radical praxis by 'overturning,' 'displacing,' and 'transgressing' the binary oppositions of metaphysics.[100]

As we saw earlier, the salient features of tactical political philosophy – which we have, with Todd May, identified as a kind of anarchism – are four-fold. First, tactical political philosophy denies any *substantial* distinction between liberatory and oppressive power structures; power is capable of giving rise to either liberation or oppression depending upon a complex array of conditions. Second, tactical political philosophy denies that power as such (whether understood as the Derridean play of differences or as the Deleuzean flow of desire) can in some sense be 'abolished' as a condition of political emancipation. Third, tactical political philosophy denies, contra Marxism and certain forms of feminism, that oppressive power emanates from a unitary source. Instead, it argues that such power emerges at multiple local sites and must be resisted at those sites accordingly. Fourth, and finally, tactical political philosophy avoids teleological or utopian discourses as foundations for political praxis.

The question, of course, is whether Derrida's work prior to 1994 may be understood in this vein, and I think we have already provided ample evidence that it can. To begin with, Derrida repeatedly insists that oppressive binary structures are an *effect* of linguistic play – they are not arbitrarily imposed (though he often speaks of them as being imposed). Political liberation, for Derrida, is indeed a consequence of the collapse and dissolution of these structures, but any such liberation is produced by the very same forces which gave rise to oppression in the first place. Put another way, *différance* undoes the same oppressive binary oppositions to which it occasionally gives rise. In this sense Derrida is very much of a piece with Deleuze, for whom desire always contains both revolutionary and fascist inclinations which manifest themselves variously.

Derrida further insists that *différance*, like Deleuzean desire, is not a thing in the world so much as a 'process' or 'event' which gives rise to or produces things in the world. To this extent it is both ubiquitous and constitutive; it cannot be 'done away with' in favor of something else. This is not to say, however, that oppression is inevitable or that it cannot be resisted when it occurs. Though he is by no means clear on this score, Derrida does seem to think that the transgressive, liberatory operation of *différance* can in some sense be 'channeled' at the level of practice – in Deleuzean terms, deterritorialization or escape along lines of flight *is* a possibility, and the actualization of this possibility is not necessarily a product of mere chance or coincidence.

As we saw earlier, moreover, Derrida repeatedly denies that oppressive binary oppositions emerge at a unitary locus (e.g., capitalism, patriarchy, etc) that can be identified and combated. There is no 'macrofascism' to which all 'microfascisms' can be reduced; rather, oppressive structures are identified solely in terms of their attempts to instantiate presence, to impose stasis upon the play of language, and this can and does happen within multiple sites. As with Deleuze, this necessitates a praxis which is always and already *local* in orientation; the emancipatory collapse of an oppressive structure at one site quickly gives rise to the generation of a new structure at another site. Thus political praxis must be dynamic, fluid, and eternally vigilant.

Lastly, Derrida's political philosophy consistently spurns teleological or utopian discourses as a foundation for praxis, as any such discourses inevitably reproduce the structures they aim to oppose. It is this insight, more so than any other, which underlies later works such as *Spectres of Marx* – specifically the all-important concept of the 'to come' (*la venir*) articulated therein.[101] For Derrida, as for Deleuze and Foucault, the revolution necessarily lacks a *telos* or *eschaton* and so must be in some sense *eternal*. In the place of justice and democracy Derrida emphasizes justice and democracy 'to come.' Freedom is not a goal so much as a practice or process that is immanent to the struggle against un-freedom. Anarchism emerges as the condition of possibility for engaging in this open-ended and free-floating 'practice of freedom' which does not, and need not, culminate in a utopian 'end of history.'

All of this is by way of saying that Derrida's earlier deconstructive works do evince a meaningful political content – one that is decidedly anarchistic in orientation. One could argue, as I in fact do, that the works that emerged during his so-called 'political turn' are mere elaborations on themes which are present throughout his career. But does Derrida's political philosophy entail a conception of normativity? This is an important question, as we saw in the case of Deleuze. For without some motivating ground for political praxis, there is no reason in principle to reject oppressive structures in favor of liberatory structures, and the oft-repeated accusation of moral nihilism is vindicated.

Before we can answer this question, it behooves us to make certain distinctions which were overlooked in the previous section on Deleuze. Modern philosophy is accustomed to conflating normativity as such with a specific *brand* of normativity which is associated mostly with Kant. That brand of normativity, which I call *nomological normativity*, emphasizes rational and universalizable laws (read: 'norms') which are taken to govern (or be governable over) human behavior. This is the kind of normativity which Todd May attributes, mistakenly I think, to Deleuze. I would argue that Derrida rejects this conception of normativity for similar albeit distinct reasons. In the first place, there is no such thing as a fixed, timeless, and ahistorical conception of human rationality for Derrida. Such a conception is merely one of a host of totalizing binary structures which deconstruction disrupts. Furthermore, the nomological conception of universalizability necessarily presupposes a static and self-transparent subject (often referred to as the 'Cartesio-Kantian' subject) which in turn presupposes a virulent form of the metaphysics of presence. Derrida specifically denies that such subjects exist, thus he denies that there are universal categories which apply absolutely and unequivocally to all of them.

At the same time, however, there is perhaps *another* conception of normativity which we might term *ontological normativity*. The best example of this form of normativity is arguably Levinas' notion of infinite ethical responsibility. According to this notion, ethical obligation *precedes* being and so is not defined in terms of the modal properties of beings; it is, in other words, a 'thou must' which takes no account of a 'thou can'.[102] For Deleuze, of course, ethics is immanent to ontology so whatever ontological normativity exists at the level of reality is coextensive with reality. (Paul Patton argues that ontological normativity for Deleuze involves the drive to 'absolute deterritorialization,' a concept that is similar to Spinoza's *conatus*, but I shall not pursue this here.[103]) In the case of Derrida, however, no specific ontology is provided, thus it is difficult to say what the relationship between ethics and ontology is supposed to be for him.

This is not to say, however, that there isn't *something* like ontological normativity in Derrida. One could argue, as I have elsewhere, that the operation of *différance* is itself guided by a kind of normativity, in the sense that *différance* must always and already overcome the linguistic and conceptual structures which emerge around it. Though it is true that *différance* is a process or event within *language*, language manifests (as we saw earlier) at the level of a praxis – hence, at the level of being. Moreover, the relationship between language and the structures within which language manifests itself is immanent and reciprocal. For this reason, it seems right to say that *différance* operates within the field of praxis *as well*, and to this extent can be construed as a kind of ontological normativity. The same operations of *différance* which alternately produce and dismantle linguistic and conceptual structures also produce and dismantle the political practices and institutions which embody them. In this sense, *différance* is something like a dialectic without *Aufhebung* – a movement of spirit which lacks any sort of teleological destiny.

This is, I readily admit, a somewhat questionable point given Derrida's persistent refusal to regard *différance* as an ontological category. As such I will let it stand as an open hypothesis. But the question remains: in lieu of nomological normativity, in what does the practical foundation of Derridean anarchism consist? Regrettably it is next to impossible to find an answer to this question in Derrida's earlier work. Prior to *Spectres of Marx* Derrida did not produce anything comparable to Foucault's *History of Sexuality* (volumes 2 and 3) or Deleuze and Guattari's *Capitalism and Schizophrenia*, so the issue of self-self/self-other relations is seldom discussed, if it is discussed at all. For this one would have to look to Derrida's later works, but these fall beyond the scope of this paper.[104]

It is worth noting, however, that the ethical framework of the later works is much more indebted to Levinas than to Nietzsche and the Greeks. To this extent, it does not rely in any obvious way upon aretaic concepts such as 'excellence' or 'care of the self' but on normative concepts such as obligation, responsibility, and hospitality. (This is also owing, of course, to the perpetually ambiguous status of the individual subject in Derrida's work. Absent a clear conception of what it means to be a subject, it is obviously difficult for Derrida to articulate anything comparable to 'becoming minor' in Deleuze or 'care of the self' in Foucault.)

As we have seen, Derrida, like Deleuze, jettisons nomological normativity in his early works, and we have every reason to believe he maintains this stance in the later, Levinas-inspired ethical works. But this doesn't mean that works like *Of Hospitality* adopt a thoroughgoing ontological normativity which places the ethical prior to the metaphysical. In point of fact, the normative status of concepts such as 'hospitality' remains a subject of fierce debate within Derrida scholarship, and I shall not discuss it here.

In sum, it is clear that Derrida's work on deconstruction affirms the tactical orientation which May associates with poststructuralist anarchism. Though the role which normativity plays in this work is perhaps somewhat more nebulous than in Deleuze, the groundwork has at least been laid for future analyses. In the meantime, there can certainly be no doubt that Derrida is a philosopher of radical liberation. Deconstructive philosophy, like Deleuzean philosophy, is one which seeks to avoid closure, entrapment, and structure; it seeks to open up rather than foreclose possibilities, to liberate rather than interrupt the flows and movements which produce life. To this extent, it is rightfully called an anarchism – not the utopian anarchism of the nineteenth century, perhaps, but the provisional and preconditional anarchism which is, and will continue to be, the foundation of postmodern politics.

The author is grateful to Sharif Gemie and the reviewers of Anarchist Studies for their helpful critiques of, and suggestions for, earlier drafts of this paper.

NOTES

1. For an exhaustive study of early French anarchist movements, see J. Maitron, *Histoire du movement anarchiste en France (1880-1914),* 2nd ed (Paris: Société universitaire d'éditions et de librairie, 1955) ; and *Le Mouvement Anarchiste en France,* Vols. 1-2 (Paris: Maspero, 1975). See also D. Berry, *History of the French Anarchist Movement, 1917-1945* (Westport, CT: Greenwood Press, 2002).

2. On the influence of anarchism within the student movement, see K.J. Heinemann, *Put Your Body Against the Wheels: Student Revolt in the 1960s* (Chicago: Ivan R. Dees, 2001).

3. See T. Nairn, 'Why it Happened,' in A. Quattrochi & T. Nairn, *The Beginning of the End: France, May 1968* (London: Panther Books, 1969).

4. This is confirmed by one of the best-known members of the French Anarchist Federation, Maurice Joyeux, in an interview in *Le fait public* 14 (January 1970), p.40.

5. Though some scholars have noted the tacit or subterranean influence of earlier movements such as Proudhonism and anarcho-syndicalism. See for example, J. Julliard 'Syndicalisme revolutionnaire et revolution etudiante', *Esprit* 6-7 (June-July 1968); G. Adam, 'Mai, ou les lecons de l'histoire ouvriere,' *France-Forum* 90-91 (October-November 1963); M. Reberioux, 'Tout ca n'empeche pas, Nicholas, que la Commune n'est pas morte,' *Politique aujourd'hui* 5 (May 1969); A. Kriegel, 'Le syndicalisme revolutionnaire et Proudhon,' in *L'actualite de Proudhon* (Brussels: l'Institut de Sociologie Libre de Bruxelles, 1967).

6. The Situationist International was a collective of radical artists whose art and

propaganda did much to shape the overall spirit of the uprisings. The two principal texts of situationism, both originally published in 1967, are G. Debord, *The Society of the Spectacle* (Detroit: Black and Red, 1983) & R. Vaneigem, *The Revolution of Everyday Life* (London: Left Bank Books, 1994). For more on the situationists and the *Enragés* more generally, see R.Viénet, *Enragés and Situationists in the Occupation Movement, France, May '68* (New York & London: Autonomedia/Rebel Press, 1992).

7. Qtd. in A. Hirsch, *The French New Left: An intellectual history from Sartre to Gorz* (Boston: South End Press, 1981), p. 143.

8. Interview with D. Cohn-Bendit in *Magazine Litteraire* 8 (May 1968).

9. For some of the situationists' criticisms of classical anarchism, see Vienet, pp.260-61.

10. D. Guerin, 'Mai, une continuitie, un reaouveau,' in *Le Fait public* 6 (May 1969); J. Maitron, 'Anarchisme,' in *La mouvment social* 69 (October-December 1969).

11. For more on the history of May 1968 and its influence, see D. Caute, *Sixty-Eight: The Year of the Barricades* (London: Paladin, 1988); R. Fraser, et al., *1968:A Student Generation in Revolt* (London: Chatto & Windus, 1988).

12. H. Hamon, '*68 – The rise and fall of a generation?*' in D.L. Hanley & A.P. Kerr, eds., *May'68* (London: The Macmillan Press, 1989), p. 20.

13. Hamon, p. 17.

14. J.E. Decker, 'Direct democracy and revolutionary organization in the 1968 French student-worker revolt,' in *Proc. of AMWSFH* 5 (1977), pp. 406-414

15. Decker, p. 407.

16. Hamon, p. 17.

17. P. Patton, *Deleuze and the Political* (New York: Routledge, 2000), p. 4; cf. G. Deleuze & F. Guattari, 'Deleuze et Guattari s'expliquent...,' *La Quinzaine Littéraire* 143:16-30 (June 1972), p. 15; cf. A. Feenberg & J. Freedman, *When Poetry Ruled the Streets: The French May Events of 1968* (Albany: SUNY Press, 2001), p. xviii.

18. Patton, p. 4.

19. G. Deleuze & F. Guattari, *Anti-Oedipus: Capitalism and Schizophrenia* [1972], trans. R. Hurley, M. Seem, & H.R. Lame (New York: Viking Press, 1977). Though we ought not to underestimate Guattari's contributions to this and later works in political philosophy, I will only refer to Deleuze in the present essay for purposes of clarity and convenience.

20. G. Deleuze & F. Guattari, *A Thousand Plateaus* [1980], trans. B. Massumi (Minneapolis: University of Minnesota Press, 1987).

21. See, for example, *Spectres of Marx*, trans. P. Kamuf (London: Routledge, 1994); *Cosmopolitanism and Forgiveness* (London: Routledge, 2001).

22. B. Foley, 'The Politics of Deconstruction,' *Genre* 17 (Spring-Summer 1984), pp. 113-133.

23. G. Spivak & M. Ryan, 'Anarchism Revisited: A New Philosophy,' *Diacritics* (June 1978), pp. 66-79.

24. In addition to the works cited in notes 23-25 below, see, e.g., R. Amster, 'Anarchism as Moral Theory: Praxis, Property, and the Postmodern,' *Anarchist*

Studies 6:2 (October 1998), pp. 97-112; J. Carter & D. Morland, 'Anti-Capitalism: Are We All Anarchists Now?' in *Anti-capitalist Britain*, ed. J. Carter & D. Morland (Gretton, Cheltenham: New Clarion Press, 2004); J. Dempsey & J. Rowe (2004), 'Why Poststructuralism is a Live Wire for the Left,' *Radical Theory/Critical Praxis: Making a Difference Beyond the Academy?*, ed. D. Fuller & R. Kitchin (Praxis, 2004); D. Graeber, *Fragments of an Anarchist Anthropology* (Chicago: Prickly Paradigm Press, 2004); A. Koch, 'Poststructuralism and the Epistemological Basis of Anarchism,' in *Philosophy of the Social Sciences* 23:3 (September 1993), pp. 327-351; S. Sheehan, *Anarchism* (London: Reaktion Books, 2003);

25. S. Newman, *From Bakunin to Lacan: Anti-Authoritarianism and the Dislocation of Power* (Oxford: Lexington Books, 2001).

26. L. Call, *Postmodern Anarchism* (Oxford: Lexington Books, 2002).

27. T. May, 'Is Post-structuralist Political Theory Anarchist?' *Philosophy and Social Criticism*, 15:2 (1989), pp. 167-182; *The Political Philosophy of Poststructuralist Anarchism* (University Park, PA: The Pennsylvania State University Press, 1994).

28. See Spivak & Ryan, for example. See also note no. 67 below.

29. G. Deleuze, *Foucault*, trans. S. Hand (Minneapolis: University of Minnesota Press, 1988).

30. G. Deleuze, *Nietzsche and Philosophy*, trans. H. Tomlinson (New York: Columbia University Press, 1983).

31. May, *The Political Philosophy of Poststructuralist Anarchism*, p. 71.

32. *Anti-Oedipus,* p. 29.

33. *Ibid.*, p. 33.

34. *Anti-Oedipus*, p. 33.

35. G. Deleuze & F. Guattari, *Kafka: Toward a Minor Literature*, trans. D. Polan (Minneapolis: University of Minnesota Press, 1986), p. 60; cf. G. Deleuze & C. Parnet, *Dialogues*, trans. H. Tomlinson & B. Haberjam (New York: Columbia University Press, 1987), p, 133.

36. May, *The Political Philosophy of Poststructuralist Anarchism,* p. 71.

37. *Anti-Oedipus*, p. 135.

38. G. Deleuze, *Expressionism in Philosophy: Spinoza,* trans. M. Joughin (New York: Zone Books, 1990), pp. 102, 218.

39. *Anti-Oedipus*, p. xiii.

40. May, *The Political Philosophy of Poststructuralist Anarchism*, pp. 11, 47-66.

41. May, *The Political Philosophy of Poststructuralist Anarchism*, p. 11.

42. D. Weick, 'Anarchist Justice,' in H. Ehrlich, et al., eds., *Reinventing Anarchy* (London: Routledge & Kegan Paul, 1979), p. 139.

43. *Ibid*; cf. Kropotkin, p. 150.

44. B. Morris, 'Anthropology and Anarchism,' in *Anarchy: A Journal of Desire Armed* 45, pp. 35-41; cf. Rocker, p. 20; cf Proudhon: 'The economic idea of capitalism, the politics of government or of authority, and the theological idea of the Church are three distinct ideas, linked in various ways, yet to attack one of them is equivalent to attacking all of them.' (*What is Property: an inquiry into the principle of right and of government*, London, William Reeves, 1969,

p. 43); cf. Malatesta, who claims that in fighting the 'exploitation and oppression of man by man,' the anarchists likewise seek 'the abolition of private property [i.e. capitalism] and government' (E. Malatesta, 'Towards Anarchism,' in *Man!: An Anthology of Anarchist Ideas, Essays, Poetry and Commentaries*, ed. M. Graham, London: Cienfuegos Press, 1974, p. 75).

45. May, *The Political Philosophy of Poststructuralist Anarchism*, pp. 63-64.

46. *Ibid.*, p. 61.

47. J. Cohn & S. Wilbur: 'What's Wrong With Postanarchism?' *Theory & Practice* (August 31, 2003).

48. May, *The Political Philosophy of Poststructuralist Anarchism*, p. 61.

49. This is not to suggest, again, that 'repressive forces' are somehow external to desires. Rather, 'repressive force' for Deleuze refers to the extent to which desire desires its own repression. In other words, repression is always and already part of every assemblage of desire (or at least has the potential to be).

50. May, *The Political Philosophy of Poststructuralist Anarchism*, pp. 121-7.

51. *Ibid.*, p. 127.

52. May, *The Political Philosophy of Poststructuralist Anarchism*, pp. 127.

53. *Ibid.*, p. 128.

54. *Ibid.*, p. 130.

55. *Ibid.*, p. 133.

56. *Ibid.*, p. 134.

57. B. Russell, *A History of Western Philosophy* (New York: Simon & Schuster, 1976), p. 569.

58. Ironically, of course, it is precisely these sorts of oppositions that Derrida seeks to elucidate and ultimately destroy. To this extent, his reputation as a thinker can itself be read as a deconstructive idiom.

59. Jurgen Habermas is arguably the most notable figure in this milieu. See for example *The Philosophical Discourse of Modernity*, trans. F. Lawrence (Cambridge: MIT Press, 1987) & *The Theory of Communicative Action*, Vol. 1, trans. T. McCarthy (Boston: Beacon Press, 1984). See also M.H. Abrams, 'How to Do Things with Texts,' *Partisan Review* 44 (1979), pp. 566-88; K. Appel, 'The *a Priori* of the Communication Community and the Foundations of Ethics: The Problem of a Rational Foundation of Ethics in the Scientific Age,' in *Towards a Transformation of Philosophy*, trans. G. Adey & D. Frisby (London: Routledge & Kegan Paul, 1980); W.J. Bate, 'The Crisis in English Studies,' *Harvard Magazine* 85:12 (1982), pp. 46-53; M.J. Devaney, *Since at least Plato ... and other Postmodern Myths* (London: Macmillan Press, 1997); P. Dews, *Logics of Disintegration: Post-Structuralist Thought and the Claims of Critical Theory* (London: Verso, 1987); John Ellis, *Against Deconstruction* (Princeton, NJ: Princeton University Press, 1989); E.D. Hirsch, *Aims of Interpretation* (Chicago: University of Chicago Press, 1976); René Wellek, *The Attack on Literature and Other Essays* (Brighton: Harvester, 1981);

60. In my opinion very few analytic philosophers have engaged Derrida in a serious and fair-minded way. (The same is true of certain scientists, most notably Alan Sokal). As a result, much of their hostility toward him has been expressed in a tacit and uncritical manner (as, for example, when twenty

analytic philosophers actively opposed Derrida's receiving an honorary doctorate in philosophy from Cambridge in 1992). A notable exception is John Searle, whose famous exchange with Derrida is recorded in *Limited, Inc.* (Northwestern University Press, 1988). See also for example D. Novitz, 'The Rage for Deconstruction,' *Monist* 69:1 (January 1986), pp. 54-76; 69(1):54 n22.

61. See for example D. D'Souza, *Illiberal Education: The Politics of Race and Sex on Campus* (New York: Free Press, 1991); R. Kimball, *Tenured Radicals: How Politics Has Corrupted Higher Education* (Harper & Row, 1990).

62. T. Eagleton, *Walter Benjamin, or Towards a Revolutionary Criticism* (London: NLB, 1981), p. 109.

63. F. Lentricchia, *After the New Criticism* (Chicago: University of Chicago Press), p. 186.

64. G. Graff, *Literature Against Itself: Literary Ideas in Modem Society* (Chicago: University of Chicago Press, 1979); cf. E. Said, 'Reflections on Recent American 'Left' Criticism,' in *The Question of Textuality Strategies of Reading in Contemporary American Criticism* (Bloomington: Indiana University Press, 1982), p. 24.

65. See for example, G. Spivak. 'Revolutions That As Yet Have No Model: Derrida's *Limited INC*', *Diacritics*, 10 (Winter. 1980), pp. 46-49; M. Ryan, *Marxism and Deconstruction. A Critical Articulation* (Baltimore: Johns Hopkins University. Press, 1982); S. Aronowitz, *The Crisis in Historical Materialism. Class. Politics and Culture in Marxist Theory* (South Hadley: J. F. Bergin, 1981); G. Hartman, 'Criticism, Indeterminacy, Irony,' in *Criticism in the Wilderness: The Study of Literature Today* (New Haven: Yale University Press, 1980), pp. 270, 271-72.

66. Two notable exceptions are John Caputo, 'Beyond Aestheticism: Derrida's Responsible Anarchy' in *Research in Phenomenology* 19 (1988), pp. 59-73; and Saul Newman, 'Derrida and the Deconstruction of Authority' in *Philosophy and Social Criticism* 27:3 (May 2001), pp. 1-20.

67. As Barbara Foley and other critics from the 1980s repeatedly suggest.

68. Ferdinand de Saussure, 'Course in General Linguistics,' in *Literary Theory: An Anthology*, ed. J. Rivkin and M. Ryan (Malden, MA: Blackwell, 1998), pp. 77-8.

69. A false attribution, incidentally, as even Plato was aware of this relationship before Saussure. The structuralist emphasis on this point is part of a larger argument that language does not reflect the world and experience. See Alan Bass, '"Literature"/Literature,' in *Velocities of Change*, ed. Richard Macksey (Baltimore and London: Methuen, 1974).

70. Saussure 81-88; cf. Ellis, pp. 63-64.

71. J. Derrida, 'Differance,' in *Literary Theory*, 390.

72. *Ibid.*, p. 391.

73. *Ibid.*, p. 397.

74. J. Derrida, *Writing and Difference*, trans. Alan Bass (Chicago: University of Chicago Press, 1978), p. 289; *Of Grammatology,* trans. Gayatri Chakravorty Spivak (Baltimore, 1976), p. 50.

75. *Writing and Difference*, p. 280.

76. J. Derrida, *Positions*, trans. Alan Bass (Chicago: University of Chicago Press, 1981), pp. 119-20.

77. *Of Grammatology*, pp. 141-60.

78. See for example J. Derrida, *Aporias: Dying – Awaiting (One Another at) the 'Limits of Truth,'* trans. T. Dutoit (Stanford: Stanford University Press, 1993).

79. See for example J. Derrida, 'Structure, Sign and Play in the Discourse of the Human Sciences,' in *The Structuralist Controversy: The Languages of Criticism and the Sciences of Man*, ed. R. Macksey and E. Donato (Baltimore: The John Hopkins Press, 1970), pp. 247-72. (Reprinted in *Writing and Difference*.)

80. Devaney, p. 17.

81. Devaney, p. 17.

82. J. Derrida, 'Plato's Pharmacy' in *Dissemination*, trans. B. Johnson (Chicago: University of Chicago Press, 1981), p. 125.

83. *Ibid.*, p. 99.

84. 'Structure, Sign, and Play,' p. 264.

85. 'Differance,' p. 7; cf. 'Living On: Border Lines,' in *Deconstruction and Criticism* (New York Continuum Books, 1979), pp. 104-5. Derrida's use of the term 'strategic' here should not be confused with Todd May's 'strategic political philosophy.' In context, it is clear that Derrida's description of deconstruction is of a piece with May's 'tactical political philosophy.'

86. Derrida, *Positions*, pp. 41-45.

87. *Ibid.*

88. Foley, pp. 119-20.

89. Lentricchia, p. 172.

90. *Ibid.*

91. Foley, p. 120.

92. Foley, p. 121.

93. Derrida, *Margins of Philosophy*, pp. 2-4, 16.

94. *Ibid.*

95. Derrida, *Margins of Philosophy*, pp. 134-35.

96. *Ibid.*, p. 213.

97. For example, Derrida discusses 'an-archic' thought and action in *Spurs: Nietzsche's Styles* (Chicago: University of Chicago Press, 1978). See also his 'Choreographies' (*Diacritics* 12:2, 1982, pp. 66-76), which offers an analysis of the institution of patriarchy, and 'The Force of Law: The Mystical Foundation of Authority' (*Cardozo Law Review*, 11:5-6, 1990, pp. 920-1045), which offers a trenchant critique of the concept of political legitimacy.

98. Foley, p. 121.

99. 'The Yale School' refers to a group of literary theorists and philosophers at literature centered at Yale University who were highly influenced by Derrida's early (pre-1985) writings on deconstruction. The group included Paul de Man, J. Hillis Miller, Geoffrey Hartman and Harold Bloom. See H. Bloom, et al., eds., *Deconstruction and Criticism* (New York: Continuum, 1979). See also J. Arac, et al., eds., *The Yale Critics: Deconstruction in America* (Minneapolis: University of Minnesota Press, 1983).

100. Derrida, *Positions,* pp. 41, 66.

101. J. Derrida, *Spectres of Marx*, trans. P. Kamuf (London: Routledge, 1994).

102. E. Levinas, *Ethics and Infinity,* trans. R. Cohen (Detroit: Duquesne University Press, 1985), pp. 8-9.

103. See Patton, p. 9.

104. In addition to *Spectres of Marx* see, for example, *The Gift of Death* (Chicago: University of Chicago Press, 1995); *Of Hospitality* (Stanford, CA: Stanford University Press, 2000); and *Rogues: Two Essays on Reason* (Stanford, CA: Stanford University Press, 2005).

Lysander Spooner's critique of the social contract

STEVE J. SHONE

Department of Political Science
University of Northern Iowa
1227 West 27th Street
Cedar Falls, IA 50614
USA

ABSTRACT

In the writings of Lysander Spooner, the inadequacy of social contract theory is a recurring theme. Its failure leads him to an innovative and extensive critique of government in general, as well as a specific rejection of the constitution of the United States. Personal experience as a leading opponent of slavery, and, paradoxically, dissatisfaction with the ensuing imposition of government by the northern United States upon the South, convinced Spooner of the ultimate impossibility of trying to ground government on consent, which, for him, would be a necessary condition for its authority. For Spooner, legitimate government is both practically and naturally untenable.

The work of Lysander Spooner (1808-1887), the American anarchist and abolitionist, has received some renewed attention in recent years due to his interest in the concept of jury nullification.[1] Otherwise, he has essentially remained forgotten, a fact that has deprived many scholars of the opportunity to acquaint themselves with a lively and original thinker. In the present paper, I address Spooner's writings about political obligation, i.e. the justification of obedience to the government, a question that, throughout the history of political theory, has concerned liberals and anarchists in particular.[2] I describe Spooner's unhappiness with social contract theory, the similarities and dissimilarities between the ideas of Spooner and David Hume in this respect, and Spooner's ultimate conclusion that it is impossible to sanction the government of the United States.

Spooner's publications appeared as monographs, some of which are quite long. For example, *The Unconstitutionality of Slavery* has 294 pages, *The Law of Intellectual Property* has 240, and *Trial By Jury* has 224; others, however, are relatively short. Today, virtually everything written by Spooner can be found in the six-volume compilation, *The Collected Works of Lysander Spooner*, edited by Charles Shively (Spooner 1971). The most notable exception is *Vices Are Not Crimes,* which, as Smith (1992, xvii) notes, was not widely known until its republication in 1977. References in this paper are made to the editions contained in *The Collected Works*, with the exception of *Vices Are Not Crimes,* for which a citation is given to *The Lysander Spooner Reader* (Spooner 1992).

Spooner was strongly opposed to slavery and an ally and confidant of John Brown. He may have had some prior knowledge of Brown's unsuccessful 1859 attack on the federal government armory at Harper's Ferry, and he even petitioned the governor of Virginia, Henry A. Wise, to spare Brown's life.[3] Nonetheless, with respect to the US Civil War, Spooner believed the North had unfairly imposed its will on the South. His viewpoint is unique, to say the least. With the passage of time, he became more and more skeptical about the legitimacy and value of the United States government. In his earlier writings, such as *The Unconstitutionality of Slavery*, Spooner had argued that the US Supreme Court should ban slavery outright, or that Congress should outlaw it; he was no supporter of the Constitution, but he believed that it should be obeyed until it was amended or replaced. Gradually, his views changed. In later works, such as the *No Treason* series, written after the ending of slavery, he continued to rail against a government that he thought had been imposed without the people's consent, focusing much more on the need to transform the political system of the United States, arguing persuasively that government and consent are incompatible, that the US government can not be justified, and that the US Constitution is a sham.

Alexander (1950, 212, fn 52) reports being able to find copies only of *No Treason* numbers I, II, and VI. Despite the curious sequencing of the numbers, it is likely that no other volumes ever existed. In an 1871 letter, Spooner wrote that these three were 'the only copies yet published.'[4] The first two parts were published in 1867, and part VI appeared in 1870. In them, Spooner explores the meaning of government by consent, the topic of the present paper.

One of the first issues Spooner attempts to dispose of in the first volume of *No Treason* is the issue of majority rule, which he conceives of as the tyranny of the majority. One way to understand the will of the masses might be in terms of strength. However, government by consent, he says, can not mean just 'consent of the *strongest party*' (Spooner 1867a, 6). Tyrants all over the world could meet that test. This is a familiar starting point: for example, rejecting Trotsky's conclusion that 'Every state is founded on force,' the great German sociologist, Max Weber (1970, 78), defined government as the body that possesses 'the monopoly of the *legitimate* use of physical force.' Adding the requirement of legitimacy seems to strengthen the definition considerably. And how would legitimacy be obtained? Perhaps, in this day and age, by winning an election. Thus we come close to considering what Spooner is aiming for, government by consent. However, he takes pains to point out that, for him, government by consent does not mean 'consent of the *most numerous party*' (Spooner 1867a, 7). For many people, of course, majority rule, conceived as numbers rather than strength, is what democracy is all about. But minorities also have entitlements, argues Spooner. Men and women have 'natural rights' that can not be taken away by one person or a group – just because they happen to win an election. This applies regardless of whether the usurpation is 'committed by one man, calling himself a robber ... or by millions, calling themselves a government' (7). The American Revolution, after all, was a case of minority (the colonists) taking back power from the control of the majority (the British Empire); if that was justified then, as most Americans believe, minority freedom is similarly justified today (8).

Focusing now on the central issue of political obligation, Spooner asks on what authority the US government rules. He decides that the right of a nation to rule can only be established on the basis of consent. Government is justified not by strength, not by majoritarianism (the consent of the majority), but by the consent of all (9-10). Thus legitimate government requires 'the separate, individual consent of every man who is required to contribute, either by taxation or personal service, to the support of the government. All this, or nothing, is necessarily implied, because one man's consent is just as necessary as any other man's' (11). Not only must consent be universal, but it can never be assumed: 'for if a man has never consented or agreed to support a government, he breaks no faith in refusing to support it' (11). This understanding of the meaning of consent was implied by the Declaration of Independence. Here, Spooner resembles the modern writer, Robert Paul Wolff, in his book, *In Defense of Anarchism* (Wolff 1976). Wolff argues that any polity is deficient unless it is based on unanimous direct democracy – i.e., unless everyone individually consents to every law that is passed:

> Unanimity is clearly thought to be the method of making decisions which is most obviously legitimate; other forms are presented as compromises with this ideal, and the arguments in favor of them seek to show that the authority of unanimous democracy is not fatally weakened by the necessity of using representation or majority rule. (Wolff 1976, 27)

For Spooner, however, less direct forms of democracy *are* 'fatally weakened.' While Wolff's argument is heuristic, the purpose of his academic book being to contemplate what ideal democracy might denote, Spooner's perspective is not philosophical at all. Although, like Wolff, he concedes that it is impossible for each person to consent to every law (Spooner 1852, 132), nonetheless he insists that consent to government must be unanimous and direct.

Even if everyone were to vote in favor of a government, Spooner still has several criticisms concerning the possibility of consent. Firstly, even if a person agrees to government, Spooner argues, that submission is not a permanent undertaking. Secondly, future generations are never bound by their ancestors' consent. The US Constitution at most obligated the people who were alive at the time. Thirdly, just because you vote does not mean you consent to the government. Finally, the liberal idea of a social contract between ruler and ruled is not valid if everyone did not get to sign the document.

When Spooner talks of exercising natural rights, as he does repeatedly, this phraseology seems to fulfill the function of a state of nature in other theories. That is because, for Spooner, the foundation of consent lies in natural justice, not in a social contract at all. He speaks of the 'natural rights of property, liberty, and life' (Spooner 1882, 7), 'all men's rights being immutably fixed' (Spooner 1886, 22), 'that natural, inherent, inalienable, *individual* right to liberty – with which it has generally been supposed that God, or Nature, has endowed every human being' (1886, 30), and '*natural* rights ... that ... are the gift of God, or Nature, to him, *as an individual*, for his own uses, and for his own happiness' (1886, 30). Moreover, '[t]his right of personal liberty is inalienable. No man can sell it, or transfer it to another; or give to another any right of arbitrary dominion over him' (1886, 32). Yet, 'the government does not even recognize a man's natural right to his own life' (1886, 31), and '[t]he government recognizes no such thing as any *natural* right of property, on the part of individuals' (1886, 32). In practice, all government, including that of the United States, lacks legitimacy, and all government violates natural law.

This pessimistic conclusion causes Spooner to reject the sovereignty of governments, for the idea of a sovereignty of nations implies that the government has trampled on the natural rights of the people. European governments at the time of the American Revolution relied not on constitutional authorization to justify their rule, but on the theory of the Divine Right of Kings. Judicial interpretation of the US Constitution has brought back that immoral rationalization, he contends, and applied it to the apparently republican government of the United States, so that the quasi-Constitutional government now relies on Divine Right. These Supreme Court justices, Spooner laments, would appear never to have encountered the Declaration of Independence, nor to have divined its consequence, that Americans are a free people (Spooner 1886, 81, 84).

For Spooner, there is a natural right of sovereignty, which refers instead to the liberty of individuals to run their own lives and control their own property, subject only to the restriction that they respect the natural sovereignty of others. As a leading abolitionist, he rejects slavery on this and other grounds. Yet governments, some of which in Spooner's time continued to allow slavery, also generally deny citizens the opportunity to subsist – for example, the right to take land and work it so that they can survive. The United States government claims to own unallocated land, and prosecutes those who attempt to make use of it for their own subsistence. We live, consequently, in a polity that not only denies our natural rights, but usurps our property (Shively 1971a, 8; Spooner 1882, 4-5; Spooner 1886, 33, 86).

In fact, Spooner seems to have anticipated the predicament of many marginal individuals, a condition more common today than in the nineteenth century when he was writing. Today, in the United States, there are hundreds of thousands of people deemed unqualified for welfare or public housing, and/or unable to work due to prior criminal acts, nonconformist behavior, or unpopular personal habits, yet these people are unable to exercise their natural right to subsist. On urban streets, they are harassed by police. Vagrancy laws, and ordinances against public camping, sleeping, sitting, urinating, and panhandling, combine to make their public existence untenable, yet they have no way of escaping to a private domicile. They can live lawfully only in a kind of hell. All that is open to such persons is crime, a violation of the one obligation Spooner argues that everyone owes to his or her neighbors, which is to treat them fairly, within the bounds of natural justice:

> In asserting its right of arbitrary dominion over that natural wealth that is indispensable to the support of human life, it asserts its right to withhold that wealth from those whose lives are dependent upon it. In this way it denies the *natural* right of human beings to live on the planet. It asserts that the government owns the planet, and that men have no right to live on it, except by first getting a permit from the government. (Spooner 1886, 34)

Like Locke, Marx, and Kropotkin, Spooner describes the antisocial consequences of the development of capitalism, for now we have a class of people who live beyond the uses and protection of government. They are outcasts, living lives that are circumscribed by allegedly democratic governments, ensuring that they can not function as productive citizens. Liberals' hope that modern government would provide a safety net for all, aiding the least advantaged members of society, is shown to be a hollow pledge. Actually, many people in modern industrial society have lost the important protection that they hitherto enjoyed, one to which, for Spooner, they were entitled by natural law – the right to survive, a claim that, ironically, is better tolerated in developing nations, even as the United States and other modern governments urge its abandonment in favor of the norms of globalization.

For Spooner, such governments are 'a mere cabal of ignorant, selfish, ambitious, rapacious, and unprincipled men, who know very little, and care to know very little, except how you can get fame, and power, and money, by trampling upon other men's rights, and robbing them of the fruits of their labor' (Spooner 1886, 24). They know no limits to their power. For example, in an argument presented in a publication of the Massachusetts State Senate, Spooner attempts to defend his friend, Thomas Drew, who refused to testify before a joint committee of the Massachusetts Legislature (Shively 1971d, 4). In that journal, Spooner attacks legislative hearings in general, viewing them as violating natural justice. From what authority, he asks, do legislatures derive the power to summon individuals to 'tell everything they may know of their neighbors and fellow-citizens' (Spooner 1869, 18)? A government that compels such tale telling, in the absence of any kind of consent to the practice, can only be 'a thoroughly infamous and detestable one' (18).

Liberty is inalienable, Spooner tells readers of *A Letter to Grover Cleveland*, and people can never give up their right to enjoy it, even voluntarily. Thus there can be no such thing as a social contract, because liberty is personal and inalienable, and can never be surrendered under any circumstances whatsoever.

Consequently the claims of others that liberty has somehow been delegated to the government are nothing but lies (Spooner 1886, 27). A social contract is impossible, according to Spooner, because it would violate natural law:

[A]ll *lawmaking* governments whatsoever – whether called monarchies, aristocracies, republics, democracies, or by any other name – are all alike violations of men's natural and rightful liberty. (Spooner 1886, 28)

Indeed, such a contract would inevitably be a fraudulent one:

To say, as the advocates of our government do, that a man must give up *some* of his natural rights, to a government, in order to have the rest of them protected – the government being all the while the sole and irresponsible judge as to what rights he does give up, and what he retains, and what are to be protected – is to say that he gives up all the rights that the government chooses, *at any time*, to assume that he has given up; and that he retains none, and is to be protected in none, except such as the government shall, at all times, see fit to protect, and to permit him to retain. This is to suppose that he has retained no rights at all, that he can, at any time, claim as his own, *as against the government*. It is to say that he has really given up every right, and reserved none. (Spooner 1886, 13)

In his history of American anarchism, James J. Martin says of Spooner's rejection of social contract theory:

> Spooner in a prominent sense was engaged in reviving the stand of the critics of Thomas Hobbes and the social contract theory, who held that the only persons bound to such an agreement were those actually participating in a pact of submission to a ruler. (Martin 1970, 194)

Although Spooner does not mention Hobbes or Locke, the modern reader is bound to associate them with social contract theory. As Martin appears to recognize, Spooner's criticisms hit Hobbes hard; however, whether or not they apply fully to Locke, who had a much greater influence on the thought underlying the American Revolution than did Hobbes, is a different question.

For Hobbes ([1651] 1981, 185-86), the state of nature is a condition of permanent war against other people, even at times when war is not literally taking place. To end this conflict, he argues that people should agree to sacrifice some rights, in order to put an end to the uncertainty and conflict. Government thus becomes a tonic for constant suspicion, anxiety and war, as Hobbes explains its development as a transition from a state of nature, via a social contract, toward a more ordered form of civilization.

In the simple society that is represented by the state of nature, people are responsible for themselves. If they need food and clothing, they go out and try to find something appropriate that can serve this function. Maybe this involves killing deer, or gathering apples, or discovering a source of water. Maybe it involves taking something from a neighbor. Following Hobbes' compact, people lay down their rights to live in this unfettered way, to just go out and appropriate what they can. Upon signing the covenant, the people make themselves subjects of the sovereign. A social contract will not work unless it is enforced, so the signers give up their power to the state, who is to be Leviathan, a frightening brute, who will scare the citizenry into obedience. Although Hobbes believed in monarchy, the theory works just as well with any other type of government. Moreover, although the sovereign will possess all the power, it is to be used to establish and maintain security and peace on behalf of the citizens. Hobbes recognizes there is going to be a problem if the sovereign turns out to be a tyrant. But he is equally sure that the results of despotism will be better than life during the English Civil War that he lived through (Hobbes [1651] 1981, 238).

Not so John Locke, who, in *Two Treatises of Government*, describes Hobbes' medicine as being worse than the disease it seeks to cure:

> This is to think that Men are so foolish that they take care to avoid what Mischiefs are done to them by Pole-Cats or Foxes, but are content, nay think it Safety, to be devoured by Lions. (Locke 1965, 372)

For some writers, the state of nature in Hobbes is 'hypothesized' (Macpherson 1962, 18-20) or 'a methodological device' (Lemos 1978, 3). Alternatively, both Hobbes and Locke may be thinking about genuine Native American societies when they visualize it. Locke (1965, 397), like Hobbes, desires to leave 'an ill condition.' However, he does not believe that the state of nature is necessarily a state of war. He is more optimistic, trusting that even banks and other economic institutions could operate prior to the contract. Locke, like Hobbes, considers it acceptable that we give up our liberty when we enter into organized society. For Locke, like Hobbes, the process can be understood as involving *two* contracts, the first to associate and leave the state of nature, the second being an agreement between the government and the citizens that consents to the new regime. Goldsmith (1966, 140) points out that this is a structure common to the social contract theorists, including Pufendorf and Rousseau, as well as Locke. However. it can be argued that the framework does not fit Hobbes' theory so well, for, in his model, the sovereign is not actually a party to the second contract.

As was noted above, Locke, unlike Hobbes, does not identify the solution with the rule of a single sovereign. For Locke (1965, 369), the existence of a tyrant would imply people were still living in the state of nature. For, unlike Hobbes, Locke sees people as desiring not only security but also property and felicity, and a contract that will promote these goals too. Unlike, Hobbes, Locke is going to emphasize consent as the basis of all legitimate government.[5]

In recent years, political theorists have been giving more attention to the political ideas of the Scottish philosopher, David Hume. Central among these is Hume's rejection of social contract theory. Interestingly, Hume's ideas, recently reemphasized, somewhat resemble those of Spooner, which are not well known.

In his essay called 'Of the Original Contract,' Hume argues that social contract theory exaggerates the idea that government is based on consent. Recent governments may have originated with consent, but that concurrence was surely limited. He talks about the Glorious Revolution of 1689, which Locke and others tried to effect, and notes that most of the ten million people in Britain at that time took no part in the decision to bring in new monarchs, William and Mary. Other governments, however, do not even make a claim to consent:

> Were you to preach, in most parts of the world, that political connexions are founded altogether on voluntary consent or a mutual promise, the magistrate would soon imprison you as seditious. (Hume 1994, 189)

In fact, Hume says, in the past, many governments were probably set up in time of war, to organize resistance to an outside enemy. Furthermore, even if the English monarchy of 1689 did happen to be based on consent, that does not mean that any contemporary government is based on consent. 'Obedience or subjection becomes so familiar, that most men never make any inquiry about its origin or cause.' (Hume 1994, 189) This is particularly true in the Persia, China, France and Spain of his day, says Hume. Maybe even in more liberal nations such as England and Holland, it is true also. The preponderance of examples shows that consent can not be an important foundation for government (189).

Rather, Hume says, democracy is an idealistic framework. It assumes that all people have the ability to decide what is best for them, what is in their interest. But it may not be apt, for most citizens may not want to be involved in political decision-making:

> When we assert, that all lawful government arises from the consent of the
> people, we certainly do them a great deal more honour than they deserve,
> or even expect and desire from us. (Hume 1994, 194)

So Hume concludes that if we ground government in consent, a very low bar will have to suffice to be able to justify contemporary regimes. For example, we might have to argue that the fact a person did not flee a country somehow obliges him or her to accept its laws and rulers. Actually, Hume points out, the real nature of political power is such that nobody even has the ability to leave without a note from the government, otherwise known as a passport (193).

Ultimately, Hume's solution to the question of political obligation is that people should obey authority because, if they do not, society may be hurt, or the government may even break down. As Sir Ernest Barker (1960, xlii) has observed, that is 'hardly a satisfactory answer, at least for many political theorists.'

Cordato and Gable (1984, 282) note that Spooner resurrects a criticism that Hume has made of social contract theory. In fact, Spooner's arguments both resemble and differ from those of Hume. Spooner applies social contract theory to US historical circumstances, arguing that even if the American Revolution and US Constitution were based on consent, the US Civil War has taught us something else – that the US government no longer enjoys such popular assent, for the North has conquered the South. Mirroring Hume's historical examples of the absence of consent in contemporary nations, Spooner (1882b, 7) points out that Congress does not require people to read all the many volumes of laws that it has passed – just, 'at the point of a bayonet, to obey.'

For Spooner, nevertheless, unlike Hume, it is wrong to obey the government in order to prevent society from breaking down. Rather, everyone must behave in accordance with natural justice, and this involves respecting the natural rights of other people to live their lives as they see fit. Any government that fails to obey natural law lacks legitimacy. And since governments today, including the United States government, do not rule in accordance with natural justice, they should be disobeyed. Furthermore, since, for Spooner, sovereignty is an attribute of individuals, not of groups, the breaking down of society becomes irrelevant. What matters is that individuals be able to keep their liberty.

Spooner maintains that if you never consented to support a government, than you are doing nothing wrong by refusing to back it. He contends that the Declaration of Independence establishes the reasonableness of this view, because even liberals and conservatives accept the validity of that document. Here, we see further divergence from Hume. Like Locke, and unlike Hume, Spooner insists that government must be based on consent. However, like Hume, Spooner points out that it never really is.

In Spooner's writings, the social contract theorist who is criticized by name is not Hobbes or Locke, but John Marshall. Spooner was a defender of the Contract Clause, the part of Article I, Section 10 of the Constitution that says, 'No State shall ... pass any ... Law impairing the Obligation of Contracts.' He is critical of Marshall's opinion in *Ogden v. Saunders*,[6] in which the Chief Justice argued that a New York state bankruptcy law was constitutional, and not violative of the constitutional protection of contracts when it granted relief to debtors who had agreed, in a contract, to reimburse those who had lent them money.

In this opinion, we find the social contract as understood by Marshall, who contends that, in the state of nature, a need to enforce an agreement to split an animal carcass or barter food for clothing, necessitates the use of force. The justification for bolstering contracts thus lies in ancient history, before society was organized, as does the obligation for there to exist a contract that was violated in order to be permitted to utilize force. As Marshall notes, 'The rightfulness of coercion must depend on the pre-existing obligation to do that for which compulsion is used.' Following a social compact, living in society, Marshall argues, people retain an 'intrinsic' right to contract, but the concomitant permission to enforce agreements is something they have now surrendered to the government or to the courts. Similarly, the state also now enjoys the power to regulate or prohibit contracts, for laws are passed by states, and states enjoy sovereignty, unless they violate the Constitution.

Whereas, prior to society, individuals were 'free agents,' with a right to enforce the terms of broken contracts to which they were a party, Marshall contends that members of an organized society can no longer preserve this right, because to do so would undermine the peace that a social contract has produced. 'Obligation and remedy, then, are not identical,' says Marshall, because 'the first is created by the act of the parties, the last is afforded by government.' Article I, Section 10, he argues, protects the right of individuals to make a contract, but not the right to enforce it, which is today a matter for the government.

As might be expected, Spooner emphatically rejects Marshall's social contract theory as expressed in *Saunders*. For him (Spooner 1886, 64), leaving contract enforcement to the state and to state laws is to deny that agreements between people entail 'natural obligation.' If that is correct, he insists, and people do not have to do what they promise to do, Marshall's thesis is self-contradictory, because what then would be the rationale for state interference? Additionally, Spooner argues that Marshall has opened a door that will ultimately undermine the original purpose of the Contract Clause, the right to protect private property from government interference, which is 'a natural right of individuals,' that can never be taken away (Spooner 1875, 30). As a member of the Virginia delegation to the Constitutional Convention, Marshall was familiar with the disagreements that led to the Bill of Rights being added to the Constitution following ratification. Yet, Spooner contends, as the leader of the Supreme Court for decades, its great organizing force, the Chief Justice ignored and violated the same natural rights that are alluded to in the first eight amendments to the Constitution.[7] Indeed, in none of the cases that were heard in the thirty-four years of the Marshall Court, was any mention ever made of the Ninth Amendment.[8]

For Spooner (1886, 93), Marshall's theory implies that the safety promised by the social contract obligates the surrender of property rights. The position has thus become the following: 'now that these governments have, *by your own consent*, got possession of all your natural rights, they have an *'unquestionable right'* to withhold them from you forever' (95), meaning that the government of the United States has violated people's natural rights. In fact, Spooner (58) notes that *none* of the seven US Supreme Court justices participating in *Saunders* wrote in favor of an unfettered natural right to contract as visualized in the Contract Clause. In the following passage, where 'A' stands for society, and 'B' for a person signing a social contract, he concludes:

> This is as much as to say that, if A can but induce B to intrust his (B's) property with him (A), for safekeeping, under a pledge that he (A) will keep it more safely and certainly than B can do it himself, *A thereby acquires an 'unquestionable right' to keep the property forever, and let B whistle for it!* (Spooner 1886, 94-95)

This raises the question of under what circumstances a social contract might be dissolved. For Hobbes ([1651] 1981, 230), it is something like the A and B situation that Spooner describes above – even if the sovereign violates the obligation to rule in the interest of his or her subjects, there is no way to return to the state of nature (Hinnant 1977, 66; McNeilly 1968, 231, 241). For Locke, however, whose influence is more keenly felt on the US Declaration of Independence, this is precisely the sort of situation in which a society might revert to the state of nature, when the letter of a constitutional protection of individuals is ignored to promote the interest of a state government. So, we are bound to ask, is it a Hobbist straw man that is being attacked here in the guise of Marshall, because what influence did Hobbes, rather than Locke, have on the American Revolution? For Locke, a government that no longer rules on the basis of consent can be overthrown. This is the philosophical basis of the American Revolution, after all. In fact, Spooner himself relies on this theory when, looking to the American Revolution to make his argument, he asserts a natural right to revolution that can never be rescinded. In the following passage, from *No Treason, No. 1,* Spooner interprets the American Revolution as a Lockean vehicle, not a Hobbesian one.

> Thus the whole Revolution turned upon, asserted, and, in theory, established, the right of each and every man, at his discretion, to release himself from the support of the government under which he had lived. And this principle was asserted, not as a right peculiar to themselves, or to that time, or as applicable only to the government then existing; but as a universal right of all men, at all times, and under all circumstances. (Spooner 1867a, 13)

Nonetheless, the social contract theory expounded by Marshall in *Ogden v. Saunders* is surely the view of Hobbes, and not that of Locke. For Hobbes believed that, once the covenant has been enacted, individuals are no longer the judge of what is right or wrong, or true or false. Moreover, for Hobbes, sovereignty is forever. And, for Spooner, the problem is that once you have a government, you can not stop it behaving like Leviathan, taking away constitutional protections in the way that Marshall does in *Saunders* – which was Locke's reason for making his quip about polecats and lions, a concern that Hobbes considered, but failed to adequately address. So the irony lies in the fact that Spooner is criticizing social contract theory using an argument made by Locke and contemplated by Hobbes. Despite his stated opposition to basing government on a social contract, Spooner accepts the part of Locke's argument that says that, if the government does not rule by consent, it is legitimate for the people to seek to replace it. If Spooner is correct in his characterization of the federal government, as personified by Marshall in *Saunders*, the US government is no longer based on consent. In fact, he goes even further than this, arguing that no government could ever be based on consent, for it is 'naturally impossible' (1886, 104). Clearly, this an anarchist position, for, although anarchism and classical liberalism start with a similar skepticism about the possibility of political obligation, liberals tend to find modern governments justified by consent, whereas anarchists remain unconvinced. As Reichert points out in his history of American anarchism:

> If the state, which is to say, government, has the ultimate power to reverse or veto any decision made by an individual even when acting in accordance with his own rational judgement, the Liberal is forced to admit that individual rights and power are not in fact inalienable but very definitely subject to limitation by a superior sovereign force ... anarchism, unlike liberalism, cannot be criticized on the grounds that it accommodates its dedication to the principle of individual freedom to the demands of power and public order. (Reichert 1976, 3-4)

Similarly, the anarchist Rudolf Rocker contrasts the two ideologies as follows:

> Anarchism has in common with Liberalism the idea that the happiness and the prosperity of the individual must be the standard in all social matters. And, in common with the great representatives of Liberal thought, it has also the idea of limiting the functions of government to a minimum. Its supporters have followed this thought to its ultimate logical consequences, and wish to eliminate every institution of political power from the life of society. When Jefferson clothes the basic concept of Liberalism in the words: 'That government is best which governs least,' then Anarchists say with Thoreau: 'That government is best which governs not at all.' (Rocker 1989, 23)[9]

How *might* consent be manifest in the US Constitution? In *No Treason, No. II*, Spooner opens a different line of attack. By starting with a reference to 'We, the People,' the document implies the necessity of consent, or else, Spooner says, the Constitution itself would have no authority. Moreover, such an agreement clearly could have no relevance, except as between those who actually sanctioned it. So, Spooner asks, who did get to approve the Constitution? Not women, not children, not black men, certainly. And, since most states had property qualifications for voting, the majority of white men were not given an opportunity to participate either. Finally, of those few Americans who could partake in the process, some significant number declined to do so (Spooner 1867b, 3-4). The people, notwithstanding the Constitution's opening salvo, mostly have not read, and do not understand, the document that binds their lives and actions. Anyway, nobody who is alive today signed it (Spooner 1882, 9). Nevertheless, the American people are 'presumed' to have read and understood the document, to know what George Washington and the other founders intended, and to possess knowledge of constitutional law that even scholars can not agree about (Spooner 1860, 225-26; Spooner 1870, 22; Spooner 1886, 9).

The US Constitution makes no claim to be a contract. If it were a contract, Spooner argues, it would be binding only on those who were alive when it was written, whereas, in fact, all of the people alive at that time are now deceased. Therefore, the Constitution is also dead – its allotted time has expired (Spooner 1870, 3).

> [F]or what is the Constitution? It is, at best, a writing that was drawn up more than ninety years ago; was assented to at the time only by a small number of men; generally those few white male adults who had prescribed amounts of property; probably not more than two hundred thousand at all; or one in twenty of the whole population. Those men have been long since dead. (Spooner 1882, 8)

The brevity and simplicity of the US Constitution is often seen as a strength, but such qualities cause the document to be interpreted differently. Spooner turns this advantage around, making the very malleability of the Constitution a disadvantage, because it must (and does) lead to disagreement about its meaning. A lot is resting on the determination of the Constitution's authority. For Spooner continues by arguing that, since the Constitution is not, and never was, a contract, leaders of the United States have no legitimacy either (Spooner 1870, 26).

Leaving aside the question of people who were alive at the time the US Constitution was ratified, Spooner turns to the question of those who were not. The document is surely much less binding on succeeding generations of Americans. Of the Founders, Spooner remarks: 'They had no natural power or right to make it obligatory upon their children' (Spooner 1870, 3). Even though the preamble speaks of 'our Posterity,' the Founders had no intention of compelling their progeny to live by the dictates of the Constitution. Not only did the people who were personally involved in the adoption of the Constitution fail to indicate a time period for which their assent to being governed by the Constitution would be effective and perhaps bind others (Spooner 1867b, 4-5), but the Constitution gave dominion to a small, wealthy elite, while enslaving 'the poor, the weak, and the ignorant' (Spooner 1882, 9).

For Spooner, the philosophical anarchism that he takes to the limit here is literally 'no treason.' Someone like Benedict Arnold is correctly viewed as a traitor, Spooner argues, because he claimed to be a friend of the United States, even though he was not. However, the Founding Fathers can not be described as betrayers. They told the King that they rejected his authority. Similarly, the South announced that it was seceding; southerners were enemies, not traitors. And if people today disavow their allegiance to the government, they are not disloyal either (Spooner 1867b, 8).

The 1790 federal law that set hanging as the penalty for treason, and which determined that people 'owing allegiance to the United States of America' commit treason by fighting against their country begs the question, Spooner argues, because the law fails to say how allegiance comes about (Spooner 1867b, 10-11). Surely, this can not be from the happenstance of being born on United States soil? Since the Constitution purports to rest wholly on popular consent, people can not be held accountable for allegiance unless they have themselves signed a contract. Interestingly, foreigners become citizens by making a pact of this sort. Thus, the government's understanding of loyalty makes the native's predicament under the US Constitution more precarious than that of the foreign-born citizen (Shively 1971b, 4; Spooner 1867b, 11).

Nor does the authority of the document rest on its having been signed, for no one ever signed the Constitution. For it to have been viewed as a contract, copies of the Constitution would have to have been given to the signatories, and this did not happen. Moreover, no one witnessed the (non)signing of the Constitution in the way that important contracts are notarized or otherwise guaranteed by neutral parties. The Constitution, therefore, obligates nobody (Spooner 1870, 18-19, 22; Spooner 1882, 8).

What is a nation, asks Spooner, and what is the 'United States'? Surely there is nothing to which this appellation refers. People who belong to legal entities can produce the papers that show they are members or representatives, but where are the membership cards for nations? What are the insignia of incorporation into the United States (Spooner 1870, 40-41)? In response, it might be argued that a passport achieves this purpose, for it identifies a person as a member of a country. For Spooner, however, this will not do. For his point, again, is one of legitimacy. And the nation, he believes, is necessarily a counterfeit institution. There is no such thing as a country, argues Spooner, for there has never been a contract by which the people living in any particular area got together and authorized monarchs, ambassadors, or other leaders to represent them as a distinctive group. Nations, like other governmental organizations, lack legitimacy. They are names, they are myths, but they are never polities (42).

Spooner also attacks governments from the perspective of history. The ruling classes in the US, England, Ireland, and France owe their power to illegitimate land grabs (Shively 1971c, 4). In particular, he characterizes Anglo-Saxons as the enemies of the rest of humanity, siding instead with ordinary people in Ireland. Opposing the British Empire, he considers its government to be a 'confederacy of robbers and tyrants.' European landlords, he argues, are not the real owners of their land. Their ancestors mostly acquired their property by force from the rightful possessors. Just because the land theft happened a long time ago does not excuse the crime (Spooner 1880, 4, 6, 8). Consequently, he recommends reparations for victims of colonial appropriation:

> [T]hese conspirators have, *as a government,* oppressed, robbed, enslaved, and made war upon, everybody, indiscriminately – in England, Ireland, and throughout what you call 'the British Empire' – whom they could oppress, plunder, or subdue. *In this* way, then, as well as through the original robberies of the lands, they have incurred a liability to everybody, who has, *in any way,* suffered at their hands. Whenever, then, the day of settlement comes, there will be some two hundred and fifty millions of people, who will be entitled to satisfaction for the wrongs you have inflicted upon them. (Spooner 1880, 7)

In any form of indirect democracy, the social contract fails, for when Congress makes laws 'of their own device,' they are by definition assembling rules that violate natural justice. Why, Spooner asks, should Congress members possess 'the right of arbitrary dominion' (Spooner 1882, 3)? Such a power has never been delegated. To give Congress this facility – even voluntarily – is to turn the US citizen into a slave, for people can never justifiably give up their 'natural right to liberty' (Spooner 1882, 4) or cede dominion over themselves to others (Spooner 1886, 11):

> I cannot delegate to another man any right to *make* laws – that is, laws of his own invention – and compel me to obey them. Such a contract, on my part, would be a contract to part with my natural liberty; to give myself, or sell myself, to him as a slave. Such a contract would be an absurd and void contract, utterly destitute of all legal and moral obligation. (Spooner 1886, 103)

The failure of social contract theory, and of one such contract in particular, the US Constitution, to justify political obligation, leads Spooner to consider the meaning of voting. As David Miller comments:

> Spooner challenged the contractual theorists to point to the relevant acts. Voting in elections could not count, since voters' motives were many and varied, but virtually never consisted in a wish to affirm support for the Constitution; payment of taxes could not count, because it was compulsory; and so forth. (Miller 1984, 37)

For Spooner, the act of voting is never proof that a person has given consent to the government. Rather, he views voting as a chore by virtue of which an individual might try and alleviate some of the oppression of 'a government that forces him to pay money ... under peril of weighty punishments.' People, Spooner argues, start out with a government to which they never gave consent; voting is merely a minor tinkering device with which they may try to undermine the usurper's power (Spooner 1867b, 5-6). By voting, Spooner writes in *No Treason, No. VI*, a person is absolutely *not* pledging to support the Constitution. Electing a person is only giving sanction to rule for the term of office (Spooner 1870, 6-7). The right to vote does not a democracy make: 'A man is none the less a slave because he is allowed to choose a new master once in a term of years' (Spooner 1870, 24).

Spooner's fellow-American anarchist, Benjamin R. Tucker, lauded Spooner's analysis of the Constitution. Referring to *A Letter to Grover Cleveland*, he wrote:

That masterly document will tell him what the United States constitution is and just how binding it is on anybody. (Tucker 1926, 56)

Spooner's argument can be just as equally convincing for the contemporary reader. For example, in the preface to his book, *Restoring the Lost Constitution: The Presumption of Liberty*, constitutional law scholar and Spooner admirer Randy E. Barnett (2004, ix) credits Spooner's *No Treason No. VI* with implanting 'the first seed of doubt' in his mind about the US Constitution when he read the piece as an undergraduate:

When Spooner's argument on legitimacy was combined with the practice of the Supreme Court, there was nothing left to take seriously. (Barnett 2004, x)

Spooner also criticized the secrecy involved in modern balloting. The fallacy of relying on any private vote to justify the US government, he writes, is that it does not obligate the person who is elected to serve the electorate. There is no mandate. Far from it, for the ensuing contract is anonymous in nature, the justification for a person's election being that certain unknown people have cast a ballot in his or her favor. How can a politician legitimately make a pledge to anonymous voters about whom he or she knows only that they have voted? Just exactly what is the nature of the contract that is thereby made, and how can the representative commit him or herself to the electorate by such a process? Resembling a 'conspiracy' rather than an election, secret ballots are not 'authentic,' and they bestow no legitimacy upon whomever is chosen (Spooner 1870, 32-33, Spooner 1882, 5-6, Spooner 1886, 10, 21).

Here, Spooner perhaps refines observations about the meaning of voting that were made by another of the leading American Anarchists, Josiah Warren, who wrote:

> Blackstone, and other theorists, are fatally mistaken when they get 'one general will' by a concurrence of vote. Many influences may decide a vote contrary to the feelings and views of the voters; and, more than this, perhaps no two in twenty will understand or appreciate a measure, or foresee its consequences alike, even while they are voting for it. There may be ten thousand hidden, unconscious diversities among the voters which cannot be made manifest till the measure comes to be put in practice; when, perhaps, nine out of ten of the voters will be more or less disappointed, because the result does not coincide with their particular, *individual*, expectations. (Warren 1852, 24-25)

Why do people vote for candidates who are unlikely to win? A lot of citizens vote for losers. This, Spooner argues, suggests that they are worried about the danger of election victors imposing tyranny 'under color of the Constitution' (Spooner 1870, 9). Some of those votes are protest votes – people opting for candidates who have no possibility of winning. Why would people vote for obvious also-rans? Because, Spooner says, they are dissatisfied with the political system, not because they have any desire to indicate their support for it by voting (10).

Spooner understood property as an inalienable right, the sole exception to which was that assets could be forfeited to compensate another person for damage done to him or her or to their possessions (Spooner 1886, 33). Thus, any attempt by governments to interfere in the allocation of resources violates natural justice. As was noted earlier, the inclusion of the Contract Clause in the US Constitution is, from Spooner's perspective, proof that the Founders intended to preserve a natural right to make contracts. These two natural rights are clearly interconnected, since contracts are the means by which property is bought, sold, and otherwise transferred (54-55, 58-60).

Spooner argues that people should be able to make contracts before they reach twenty-one years old, not as states have historically restricted them in this way, because he believes that many people are intellectually capable of making decisions before they reach states' artificially high ages of majority. He protests the fact that married women have been denied by state laws the ability to make contracts, because this also violates the natural rights of property and contract, not to mention the Constitution. The Constitution being gender-neutral, the appropriate standard of natural justice to be applied here is whether or not a person is mentally competent to make an assessment of circumstances (Spooner 1886, 61).

Nevertheless, individual rights might be limited if they cause undesirable societal consequences. For example, he suggests that a person who becomes violent when he or she drinks alcohol could legitimately be refused a beer (Spooner 1875, 34-35).

Since the government of the United States lacks legitimacy, the actions of its officers are without authority, and the people are entitled to resist them. For Spooner, resigning oneself to the deeds of an illegitimate government would violate the spirit of the Constitution, of which the Second Amendment anticipates the need of the populace to stand firm. What sense would it make, he asks, to give citizens the right to bear arms, but not allow them to use them against an immoral government? It may often be possible to overcome corrupt leadership without violence, but this will not always be the case, and the Second Amendment recognizes this reality. People who insist that unconstitutional laws be resisted only at the ballot box, and in the meantime be obeyed, cede to the government all effective power, with the consequence that the United States does not really have limited government at all (Spooner 1850, 27-29). Given human nature, few politicians would give up power just because they had lost an election, and their term of service had come to an end. It is only fear of the power of the people, Spooner argues, and their right to bear arms, which makes politicians in the United States willing to withdraw. Without such a deterrent, they would likely focus their intentions on enriching themselves and transforming the electorate into slaves, for 'the temptations of avarice and ambition, to which they are exposed, are too great for the mere virtue of ordinary men' (Spooner 1850, 30).

Spooner's writings on political obligation confer little authority on the government of the United States, or, indeed, on any government that has ever existed. Denying that people have consented to many laws that have been enacted, and rejecting both social contract theory and the authority of the US Constitution, Spooner seeks to justify a more limited political obligation instead by reference to natural law, including the natural rights to make contracts and own property, and the right to resist a government that recognizes no bounds to its ever-increasing power.

Spooner's work is largely forgotten today. However, it is the attempt of the author of the present paper to show that his work has much substance and contemporary relevance, and that there is still value in continuing to read him.

An earlier version of this paper was presented at the 2003 annual meeting of the Pacific Northwest Political Science Association, in Vancouver, British Columbia. The author is grateful to Tim Jeske, three anonymous reviewers, and Sharif Gemie for their comments on earlier drafts

NOTES

1. Jury nullification is a term describing occasions where juries have refused to follow instructions, and have presented unexpected verdicts. Following the acquittal of O.J. Simpson, approximately five hundred scholarly articles on the topic have appeared in law journals, and, not surprisingly, a few authors have traced the practice and its validation back to Spooner. See, for example, Conrad 1998, Ostrowski 2001, Shone 2004.

2. As I note later on in the paper, liberals tend to conclude that government can be justified, while anarchists prefer to remain skeptical.

3. Brown's exploits are commemorated in the song, *John Brown's Body*. For the petition, see Lysander Spooner, writing anonymously as 'The Author of the Circular,' letter to Henry A. Wise, Governor of Virginia, November 2, 1859. Lysander Spooner manuscripts collection, Department of Rare Books and Manuscripts, Boston Public Library.

4. Letter from Lysander Spooner to the Hon. B. F. Perry dated 5 May, 1871, Lysander Spooner manuscripts collection, Department of Rare Books and Manuscripts, Boston Public Library.

5. Of course, the precise meaning of consent for Locke is the subject of intense argument; see, for example, the debate in this journal between Call 1998, and Morland and Hopton 1999.

6. *Ogden v. Saunders*. 1827. 12 Wheaton 213.

7. The first eight amendments to the United States Constitution provide for freedom of speech, assembly, and religion, as well as protection against the quartering of troops in one's house, double jeopardy, self-incrimination, unreasonable searches and seizures, uncompensated seizure of property, cruel or unusual punishment, or excessive bail or fines. They also guarantee the rights to petition the government, to be given a swift and public trial, to receive the assistance of a lawyer when accused of a crime, and to bear arms.

8. The Ninth Amendment says: 'The enumeration in the Constitution, of certain rights, shall not be construed to deny or disparage others retained by the people.'

9. This essay was also published as an appendix to Eltzbacher 1958, with a slightly different title, 'Anarchism and Anarcho-Syndicalism.'

BIBLIOGRAPHY

A reader unfamiliar with the writings of Lysander Spooner might start with *The Lysander Spooner Reader*; this is a thoughtful collection of his writings. Currently, no book-length analysis of Spooner's life and ideas has been published.

Alexander, A. John. 1950. 'The Ideas of Lysander Spooner.' *The New England Quarterly* 23:200-217.

Barker, Sir Ernest, ed. 1960. *Social Contract: Essays by Locke, Hume, and Rousseau*. London: Oxford University Press.

Barnett, Randy E. 2004. *Restoring the Lost Constitution: The Presumption of Liberty*. Princeton, NJ: Princeton University Press.

Call, Lewis. 1998. 'Locke and Anarchism: The Issue of Consent.' *Anarchist Studies* 6:3-19.

Conrad, Clay S. 1998. *Jury Nullification: The Evolution of a Doctrine.* Durham, NC: Carolina Academic Press.

Cordato, Roy, and Wayne Gable. 1984. 'Lysander Spooner, Natural Rights, and Public Choice.' *American Behavioral Scientist* 28:279-288.

Eltzbacher, Paul. 1958. *Anarchism: Exponents of the Anarchist Philosophy.* Ed. James J. Martin. Trans. Steven T. Byington. New York: Chip's Bookshop.

Goldsmith, M. M. 1966. *Hobbes's Science of Politics.* New York: Columbia University Press.

Hinnant, Charles H. 1977. *Thomas Hobbes.* Boston: Twayne.

Hobbes, Thomas. [1651] 1981. *Leviathan.* Ed. C. B. Macpherson. Harmondsworth, Middlesex: Penguin.

Hume, David. 1994. *Political Essays.* Ed. Knud Haakonssen. Cambridge, Cambridgeshire: Cambridge University Press.

Lemos, Ramon M. 1978. *Hobbes and Locke: Power and Consent.* Athens: The University of Georgia Press.

Locke, John. 1965. *Two Treatises of Government.* Ed. Peter Laslett. New York: Mentor.

Macpherson C. B. 1962. *The Political Theory of Possessive Individualism.* London: Oxford University Press.

Martin, James J. 1970. *Men Against the State: The Expositors of Individualist Anarchism in America, 1827-1908.* Colorado Springs: Ralph Myles.

McNeilly, F. S. 1968. *The Anatomy of* Leviathan. New York: St. Martin's.

Miller, David. 1984. *Anarchism.* London: J.M. Dent.

Morland, Dave, and Terry Hopton. 1999. 'Locke and Anarchism: A Reply to Call.' *Anarchist Studies* 7:51-67.

Ostrowski, James. 2001. 'The Rise and Fall of Jury Nullification.' *Journal of Libertarian Studies* 15:89-115.

Reichert, William O. 1976. *Partisans of Freedom: A Study in American Anarchism.* Bowling Green, OH: Bowling Green University Popular Press.

Rocker, Rudolf. 1989. *Anarcho-Syndicalism.* London: Pluto.

Shively, Charles. 1971a. 'Introduction' to *A Letter to Grover Cleveland, on His False Inaugural Address, the Usurpations and Crimes of Lawmakers and Judges, and the Consequent Poverty, Ignorance, and Servitude of the People.* In *The Collected Works of Lysander Spooner*, by Lysander Spooner, ed. Charles Shively. Weston, MA: M & S Press.

Shively, Charles. 1971b. 'Introduction' to *No Treason, No. II. The Constitution.* In *The Collected Works of Lysander Spooner*, by Lysander Spooner, ed. Charles Shively. Weston, MA: M & S Press.

Shively, Charles. 1971c. 'Introduction' to *Revolution: The Only Remedy for the Oppressed Classes of Ireland, England, and Other Parts of the British Empire. No. 1.* In *The Collected Works of Lysander Spooner*, by Lysander Spooner, ed. Charles Shively. Weston, MA: M & S Press.

Shively, Charles. 1971d. 'Introduction' to *Thomas Drew vs. John M. Clark.* In *The Collected Works of Lysander Spooner*, by Lysander Spooner, ed. Charles Shively. Weston, MA: M & S Press.

Shone, Steve J. 2004. 'Lysander Spooner, Jury Nullification, and Magna Carta,' *Quinnipiac Law Review.* 22:651-669.

Smith, George H. 1992. 'Introduction.' In *The Lysander Spooner Reader*, by Lysander Spooner. San Francisco: Fox & Wilkes.

Spooner, Lysander. 1850. *A Defence for Fugitive Slaves, Against the Acts of Congress of February 12, 1793, and September 18, 1850.* In Spooner 1971.

Spooner, Lysander. 1860. *The Unconstitutionality of Slavery.* In Spooner 1971.

Spooner, Lysander. 1867a. *No Treason, No. 1.* In Spooner 1971.

Spooner, Lysander. 1867b. *No Treason, No. II. The Constitution.* In Spooner 1971.

Spooner, Lysander. 1869. *Thomas Drew vs. John M. Clark.* In Spooner 1971.

Spooner, Lysander. 1870. *No Treason, No. VI. The Constitution of No Authority.* In Spooner 1971.

Spooner, Lysander. 1875. *Vices Are Not Crimes.* In Spooner 1992.

Spooner, Lysander. 1880. *Revolution: The Only Remedy for the Oppressed Classes of Ireland, England, and Other Parts of the British Empire. No. 1.* In Spooner 1971.

Spooner, Lysander. 1882. *A Letter to Thomas F. Bayard: Challenging His Right – And that of All the Other So-Called Senators and Representatives in Congress – To Exercise Any Legislative Power Whatever Over the People of the United States.* In Spooner 1971.

Spooner, Lysander. 1886. *A Letter to Grover Cleveland, on His False Inaugural Address, the Usurpations and Crimes of Lawmakers and Judges, and the Consequent Poverty, Ignorance, and Servitude of the People.* In Spooner 1971.

Spooner, Lysander. 1971. *The Collected Works of Lysander Spooner.* Ed. Charles Shively. Weston, MA: M & S Press.

Spooner, Lysander. 1992. *The Lysander Spooner Reader.* San Francisco: Fox & Wilkes.

Tucker, Benjamin R. 1926. *Individual Liberty: Selections From the Writings of Benjamin R. Tucker.* Ed. C. L. S. New York: Vanguard.

Warren, Josiah. 1852. *Equitable Commerce: A New Development of Principles as Substitutes for Laws and Governments, for the Harmonious Adjustment and Regulation of the Pecuniary, Intellectual, and Moral Intercourse of Mankind.* Reprint. New York: Burt Franklin.

Weber, Max. 1970. *From Max Weber: Essays in Sociology.* Ed. H. H. Gerth and C. Wright Mills. London: Routledge & Kegan Paul.

Wolff, Robert Paul. 1976. *In Defense of Anarchism. With a Reply to Jeffrey H. Reiman's* In Defense of Political Philosophy. New York: Harper & Row.

REVIEWS

Political Economy from Below – Economic Thought in Communitarian Anarchism, 1840 – 1914,
Rob Knowles
London & New York: Routledge, 2004
ISBN: 0415949033, xiii and 432 pp, £60

Rob Knowles declares that his purpose in this book is 'to recover the economic ideas of European communitarian anarchists of the nineteenth century and early twentieth century.' His starting point is, interestingly, that of an economist coming across references to anarchist economic ideas in recent ecological activist literature and searching back through the original literature to find the sources of the ideas.

The introduction gives a brief historical survey of the development of anarchism and makes a familiar protest at the hostile treatment of its ideas. The stream of anarchism which sees the community and individual as necessarily interdependent – i.e. 'communitarian' anarchism – is identified as the area of study, individualist anarchism of the Josiah Warren type being declared of marginal interest only. The second chapter surveys all too briefly the different schools of current economic thought and theories of the state. The intention is to illustrate the ideas of writers who might first help break the ideological hold of neo-classical economics and introduce real people and real social relations in place of its arid abstractions. Many of these – for example the Institutionalists or Neo Keynesians – are essentially statist in their assumptions, however. The work of the 'critical realism' school of Tony Lawson and others, and the work of Karl Polanyi, are emphasised as a means of showing respectively the open nature of an economy within which many agents and intentionalities are active and the social embeddedness of economic ideas. In other words 'the state' and 'the economy' are contingent social constructions and alternative arrangements are possible.

There then follow chapters forming the bulk of the book which set out the economic ideas of Proudhon, Herzen, Bakunin, Reclus, Kropotkin, Grave and Tolstoy. By far the greatest attention is paid to Proudhon, who is given four chapters and a hundred pages out of three hundred pages of text. The development of Proudhon's economic ideas is set in the context of his life and his wider proposals on society, education and the family. Material is used which is not available in English and the account is workmanlike and a good general summary of Proudhon's ideas as a whole. This is, however, almost forced on Knowles. Though he says that it is not his purpose to survey the whole range of ideas of his chosen writers, this becomes necessary, in effect, because anarchist economics cannot be separated from ideas on social structures and social and personal moralities – in Proudhon and indeed every other writer he considers.

The coverage given to Proudhon appears to result from the volume of his writings, its conceptual (or at least expressive) complexity, his penchant for system building and the sense that he was the first, capital A, Anarchist. His successors had to set their ideas out in relation to Proudhon's in a personal or posthumous dialogue. Knowles is good on the interaction between the writers he considers – Herzen, Bakunin and Tolstoy knew Proudhon, Reclus knew Herzen and Bakunin, Reclus and Kropotkin worked closely for many years with each other and with Grave. The stages of development of ideas also seems sensible with a chapter on Herzen and Bakunin taken together and another treating Reclus and Kropotkin together. Herzen and Bakunin were both promulgators of the example of the Russian *mir* or peasant commune as an ideal type of the communist principle carried out in practice, and dubious about those elements in Proudhon's systems which contained possible seeds of future government. (Bakunin claimed his anarchism was Proudhon's system 'enlarged, developed and freed of all its metaphysical, idealist and doctrinaire decoration.') Reclus and Kropotkin were both profoundly influenced by evolutionary thinking and had a scientific evidence-based mind-set. The chapters on these thinkers and that on Jean Grave again contain material not previously in English.

The economic principles that Knowles draws from his study stem from some constant principles of social organisation in all the writers concerned, though the details and their styles of writing and activist approaches differed. All based their ideas in some form of society based on freely constituted communal associations, freely federated in turn without state power. There were differences in the specificity of these arrangements – Kropotkin referred somewhat disdainfully to Proudhon's apparent wish to make the anarchist revolution by decree. Nevertheless the continuity is clear here as it is in a principle of mutualism (Proudhon), solidarity (Bakunin), mutual aid (Kropotkin), all variations on the theme of the social development of a basic need for humans to associate for common purposes and mutual assistance.

Knowles concludes that the

> tradition of [the communitarian anarchists of the nineteenth century] economic thought was internally consistent in its basic characteristics. In fundamental terms, three dimensions of a communitarian anarchist economy can be readily identified: first, the society comprised 'institutions,' freely constituted and not fixed in form or content; secondly, the economy, being embedded in society, could never be considered as separate from society, such that it could never be analysed as an abstract entity; and thirdly, an ethic was always prior to the economy in every respect. The ethic in action was the force of social cohesion.

The principle of federation of institutions flowed from these principles, as did the principle that the resources of the world, properly organised, could provide for all 'without exception and without favour or privilege' and could minimise and respect human labour. After a brief account of an extensive system of mutual aid in the slums of Lima his final words are: 'the tradition of economic thought of the communitarian anarchists has intellectual and practical utility. It is a living tradition.' (p.301)

Rob Knowles set out to recover the economic ideas of European communitarian anarchists of the nineteenth century and early twentieth century. The book is a useful addition to the literature, particularly for the material not previously in English. The implied focus on readers approaching from an economists' milieu will hopefully result in some interesting intellectual mash-ups. Those readers who are familiar with accounts of the thoughts of the anarchist sages may welcome a fresh account from a different perspective, but will not, however, particularly regard this as a recovery of anarchist economic ideas because the economic ideas are so entwined with the familiar analysis of existing societies and suggestions for a better one.

It is not a criticism of Rob Knowles – he has delivered the book he set out to write – but there is clearly a space for further work on the radical edge of economics and theory of the state touched upon in Chapter Two. The constant revitalisation of anarchist thought requires interaction with new ideas developing from action within the anarchist milieu and ideas from all sorts of sources coming in from outside. The huge influence of evolutionary ideas on Kropotkin, for example, appears almost wholly beneficial. But Kropotkin's writing is a hundred years old and more. The social landscape of control and areas of relative autonomy, issues of poverty and affluence, of education and information, of the nature of work, of the survival of the planet are all radically different now. We cannot keep returning to the sages forever.

John Quail
University of York

The British Folk Revival (1944-2002)
Michael Brocken
Ashgate, Aldershot, UK, 2003
ISBN 07546 3281 4 (Hbk), £56; ISBN 07546 32282 2 (Pbk), £17.50

As both popular entertainment and also a forum for story telling and social commentary with a long and varied history, folk music's wider popularity ebbs and flows according to a complex web of personalities, performers, media and industry investment, individual and collective effort; but, as with any 'community' endeavour, its history, although by no means a purely libertarian one, is deeply rooted in self-management. An account of 'folk music', the activities of folk clubs and the personalities involved can provide a clear insight into the ways in which people can create oases of genuinely libertarian popular culture; however, there also exist numerous examples of folkies and folk clubs developing personal powerbases, hierarchies and authoritarian formal or informal structures.

Michael Brocken's account of the post-World War II British Folk Revival provides a fascinating, opinionated and inexhaustive account of events in the world of folk music in the second half of the twentieth century. From the outset, Brocken is clear that he sees folk music as an agent of social change. Given the massive social upheaval of the era covered by the book, his attempt to locate folk music within the changes in society is ambitious to say the least.

Initially, Brocken indicates an obvious conflict within folk music. Since the activities of Cecil Sharp and his contemporaries at the turn of the twentieth century, folk music has had a tendency to recall 'Golden ages', simpler times, spiritual authenticity and now-defunct practices and people, particularly in the light of the 'loss' of those traditions in an industrial and post-industrial age. However, he also notes that, as an activity that involves performers, storytellers, and artistic creators, it is, by definition, active, current and forward-looking. Therefore, there will always exist a tension between those who are looking to recreate the 'authentic' from times past with those who believe that their very presence in the 'scene' creates a new 'authentic'. This also presents a conflict between the active folkies (those who play, sing, record, hark back nostalgically, etc.) and the passive consumers (who also play, sing, record and hark back, but just don't do it as publicly or possibly with quite so much 'authenticity'). Brocken seeks to unpick some of these conflicts, and to make explicit the influences of social class, dynamic individuals and the march of time and external social change on the post-War folk revival.

Brocken has no doubt that history is, for the most part, purely nostalgia, and quite definitely not the 'truth', and he demonstrates very clearly the role of middle-class collectors in the recording and creation of folk traditions in Britain, particularly as a defence against the advent of new recording and broadcast technologies and the threatened cultural supremacy of African-American music from the 1930s onwards. He is acutely aware of the nature of different ages to invent and repackage traditions for a variety of reasons and to tout them as 'authentic', although as a historian of social change, he also falls into the trap of assuming certain truths about history and tradition, particularly in his assumption that his experiences (of 1960s or 70s folk clubs) can be portrayed as universal, or that record sales and the activities of 'super-stars' are in any way indicative of many of the consuming or producing activities of folkies throughout the land.

A central theme of this work is the ongoing conflict between 'folk' and 'popular' as definitions of culture, and particularly working class culture as defined by middle class and state institutions such as the BBC. The failure of the BBC to recognise or cater for working class and youth pref-erences for certain types of broadcast music in the 1940s and '50s can be only perceived as bizarre from a twenty-first century perspective, given modern communications technologies, but does perhaps shed some light on the insight of contemporary social commentators' opinions, such as Orwell. Similarly, the role of Ewan MacColl and Bert Lloyd in attempting to unleash a genuinely political folk music, but only one which reflected their authoritarian and inflexible Marxist blueprints, strikes one as unfor-tunate and even ridiculous. Brocken recounts tales of such shenanigans with relish, and leaves the reader in no doubt as to his preference for a multiform, open, dynamic folk music.

As an account of social change, technological development and a small backwater of music in England (with rare forays north and west of the borders), this is a fascinating and erudite work. Exhaustive it is not – and there is something of an omission of the more explicitly libertarian end of the genre, as represented by post 1980s British radical folksters such as Chumbawamba and The Levellers – but it serves to open doors on to a wide variety of themes, using folk music as its starting point. Michael Brocken seeks to smash a few icons while outlining his own personal thesis that folk music, if it is to survive as a genre, needs to embrace capi-talism (in the form of the music industry and 'Showbiz') and 'the popular' wholeheartedly, rather than staying within its own limited ghetto.

Numerous questions are raised about the nature of 'authenticity' within folk music, but Brocken fails, in my opinion, to question some of the more fundamental issues about where the power lies within folk music and, in a wider sense, within popular culture. Clearly there are gate-keepers within the 'folk scene' as much as there are in the wider broadcast media and the music industry, who decide what is 'acceptable' or 'good', and, by defini-tion, what is not. There is a sense of hope within his book that the 'good music' will find its way into the public arena thanks to the activities of the music industry, but he fails to address the recurrent issue of who decides what music should reach a wider public, why, and by what means.

Advances in technology with regard to recording and broadcasting continue to open up new avenues for the democratic spread of music, but it still remains the case that the current folk music scene is heavily biased towards the promotion of the 'old masters', their progeny or their friends.

This may merely be evidence of meritocracy in action ('They are better musicians with better songs'), lazy promoters and journalists ('Give the public what they know and tell them they'll like it'), an undiscerning public ('We like them because we recognise their name, and because everybody else seems to like them'), or just another dynasty for which we can choose to vote for with our feet and wallets. Alternatively, we can ignore them all because we are too busy creating our own dynamic, forward-looking and genuinely radical folk music, irrespective of the constraints of tradition, good taste, perceptions of 'good art', or any other externally imposed limits.

Brocken's book additionally provides a welcome and largely extensive discography of Topic Records' releases since the 1930s, a full bibliography and an index.

This is not a particularly easy book to read, and I had to make notes throughout in order to follow his thread. However, I found it an informative, satisfying and provocative read. For anybody venturing into the genre of folk music and the issues of musical production and consumption, this is an extremely worthwhile study that poses difficult questions, and leaves the way open for plenty of future speculation. As Brocken notes, '[music is]... a vast argumentative texture through which people construct their own reality' (p.89). His ideas and experiences are partial and opinionated, but his narrative is informative and engaging and I'm sure historians and social observers of the twentieth century will be tempted to debate the themes herein long and hard over a few pewter tankards of real ale and a plate of kippers...

James 'Bar' Bowen
www.myspace.com/jamesbarbowen

Resisting Our Culture of Conformity: In the Hills of Southern Ohio and in the Groves of Academe
Wayne Burns
Blue Daylight Books, P.O. Box 805, Alpine, CA 91903. 2006.
ISBN 0-9718849-2-7 xxi + 305 pp. US$14.95

It seems safe to say that Wayne Burns is unknown in Britain and that his name is scarcely more familiar, certainly nowadays, in his native USA. Yet he was a Professor of English at the University of Washington in Seattle for over thirty years and during the 1950s and 1960s so enthused his students that many proceeded to disseminate his ideas on politics and literature in their later careers. There were, for example, north of the border, the late John Doheny at the University of British Columbia and Jerry Zaslove at Simon Fraser University, while Art Efron at the State University of New York at Buffalo and Gerald Butler at San Diego State University produced long-running periodicals, *Paunch* and *Recovering Literature* respectively, discussing and advancing parasitic anarchism and the Panzaic principle.

Parasitic anarchism can be easily explained. Burns believes it no longer possible (and clearly doubts that it ever was) to either overthrow or significantly modify the capitalist system, which controls not only the minds of its citizens but also the choices open to their minds. All that those who somehow manage to avoid this enveloping control can do is to be 'parasites on the body social and the body politic', linking up with other 'parasitic anarchists' and attempting to enjoy life to the full, while shunning all positions of power and even work that contributes to the maintenance and legitimation of the system. Burns's political theory is then a typically gloomy variant of individualist anarchism. It is however directly related to a theory of the novel that is arresting, highly original and demanding of the attention of any dedicated reader of fiction.

At the heart of the literature Burns most admires are parasitic anarchists, admittedly not self-aware but nonetheless parasitic and anarchistic: Moll Flanders; Arabella, Jude Fawley's wife, in *Jude the Obscure*; the Good Soldier Švejk; Ferdinand in Louis-Ferdinand Céline's *Death on the Instalment Plan*; Zorba the Greek; naturally Shakespeare's Falstaff; and also Sancho Panza, who gives his name to the Panzaic principle. Sancho Panza perpetually refutes, with his bodily needs, materialism and realism, the delusions and idealism of his master, Don Quixote. In a key passage of 'The Panzaic Principle' (1965), Burns's major statement of his literary aesthetic, he contends (and it will now be seen why Efron's journal was called *Paunch*) that

Sancho's belly has not only burst the seams of Venus's girdle, it has given the lie to Dulcinea and in fact all of Don Quixote's ideals – much as Lady Chatterley's guts give the lie to Clifford and his ideals in *Lady Chatterley's Lover*:

'My dear, you speak as if you were ushering it all in! [i.e., 'the life of the human body'] … Believe me, whatever God there is is slowly eliminating the guts and alimentary system from the human being, to evolve a higher, more spiritual being'.

'Why should I believe you, Clifford, when I feel that whatever God there is has at last wakened up in my guts, as you call them, and is rippling so happily there, like Dawn? Why should I believe you, when I feel so very much the contrary?'

Burns comments that 'in life the rightness of the guts (as against the mind) will depend on one's point of view'; but he believes that 'in Lawrence's as in all other novels, however, the guts are always right...' He had started out in 1951 by arguing that any 'serious' novelist was a revolutionary, 'never at one with his society and its values': 'he has to be free to function as a 'licensed madman and revolutionary' – the way all great novelists have, in fact, been obliged to function'. In 'The Panzaic Principle' he went further, maintaining that

> it is an axiom or principle of the novel that [the guts] are always right, that the senses of even a fool can give the lie to even the most profound abstractions of the noblest thinker. And this is the principle I have designated the Panzaic principle ... Idealistic critics ... generally recognize this principle, much as they hate and deplore it. They know or sense that, in fiction, the guts...are always right; this is why they want to keep them out, or cover them up, or somehow bowdlerize them.

When the full version of *The Panzaic Principle* was published in 1972 as a book it had as a frontispiece a *New Yorker* cartoon of an enormous oil painting in a gallery showing a man and woman fucking while a respectable 'little old lady' is making a copy of only the bird flying in a corner of the original (reproduced on p. 248 of the book under review). This states wonderfully well in visual form the central premise of Burns's theory – and, I would add, the way in which priests and purveyors of spirituality, politicians and ideologues, hate and sideline the everyday needs and pleasures of the ordinary human being.

In 1982 Burns brought out *Journey through the Dark Woods*, taking its title from a passage in Lawrence, always a touchstone for him – 'We can look in the real novels, and there listen in ... to the low, calling cries of the characters, as they wander in the dark woods of their destiny' – and with a foreword by Alex Comfort, one of the contemporary writers he most admired and about whose work he published several articles. This first autobiography is unusual in being exclusively concerned with his university career and intellectual development. *The Vanishing Individual: A Voice from the Dustheap of History: Or, How To Be Happy without Being Hopeful*, a full-length book although appearing in 1995 as a special issue of *Recovering Literature*, is also highly autobiographical, while expounding parasitic anarchism and Burns's analysis of fiction, including most usefully long extracts from *The Panzaic Principle* and other theoretical texts (from which I have drawn above). Reviewing it in *Freedom* (4 May 1996), Doheny ventured that it was 'possibly a great book' but, despite its considerable interest and definite utility as a guide to Burns's thought, that certainly exaggerates its achievement. Now at around the age of ninety – his birth was never registered and he doesn't know whether he was born in 1916 or 1918 – Burns has written, its title notwithstanding, a second autobiography, *Resisting Our Culture of Conformity*.

This time he has produced a complete account, melding his boyhood in hillbilly south Ohio with his *five* marriages (three of them analyzed in detail) and his life as a teacher and writer. The downside – at least for readers of the two earlier books – is that the treatment of his public career repeats much of what has already been published, with the second half of *Resisting Our Culture of Conformity* simply reprinting verbatim the bulk of *Journey through the Dark Woods*. Yet there is also much that is fresh and exceedingly attractive; and the first hundred pages on Burns's upbringing deserve to be recognized as a small classic. His father was a farmer who died when he was a toddler, his stepfather the proprietor of a series of cinemas in the tiny country towns of southern Ohio and Kentucky. He was raised by his adoring mother and her mother, with much influence from an aunt and two radical, atheist uncles, one of whom was a trade-union militant in nearby Cincinnati. Another uncle left him a library of novels that included sets of Balzac, Victor Hugo and Zola. Indeed, given the physical freedom and freethinking of his childhood, it is difficult to understand Burns's perpetual tirade against the conformity of the local people. The libertarianism extended to tolerance, even if reluctant, of the full sexual relationships of teenagers. Boys and girls spoke of being 'married' and boys of their 'wives', as in 'My wife won't be able to come to the party'. Mary was twelve and Burns probably fourteen when they entered into complete sexual union, they were eventually to be legally married and their relationship was highly successful for some fifteen years (until they were driven apart by the disdain of several academic communities, particularly the women, since she was not a graduate).

What comes initially as a surprise in Burns's books is his rancorous antipathy to the student radicalism of the late sixties and early seventies, to which he attributes the termination of the personal teaching style he'd evolved since the forties and his early retirement. He rejected the exercise of power (at least consciously) in his classes and expected in the mutual encounter with 'serious' fiction or 'great' novels – there is an obvious parallel with F.R. Leavis in both this language and the elevation of the reading of literature to the supreme good (not to mention the fervour of the disciples and the construction of a highly restricted canon of admired works) – his students as well as himself to expose their preconceptions and beliefs and be prepared to modify these, as they collectively experienced the 'hurt' (Lawrence's term again) occasioned by all 'genuine' art and recognized their own individuality. Comfort, who visited several of Burns's classes, was critical, maintaining that what was being done amounted to 'incomplete analysis', and could be really quite dangerous, since I was, as he saw it, functioning as analyst rather than teacher, and in the process was bringing the students to the point of seeing how desperate their own situations were, then leaving them to work their own way out of their dilemmas as best they could, with only a few shreds of humanistic philosophy to guide them. While I had to acknowledge an element of truth in this observation, I still maintained ... that, dangerous as the process might be, it was really the best if not the only way to help the students to a full understanding of the novels – and, through the novels, of themselves and the world they lived in.

This almost therapeutic literary criticism was derailed by the turmoil on the campus at Seattle and the various party lines, whether socialist, sexual, feminist or black power, that students now adhered to. Although the situation was to ease in the course of the seventies, Burns's methods were destined to wither in a period of increasing thought control and anti-individualism, including the political correctness which pounces on the slightest deviation from its self-generated tenets.

Burns agonizes over the forces making for conformity during his lifetime. Oddly he makes no mention of the various prominent works in postwar American sociology, such as David Riesman's *The Lonely Crowd* and William H. Whyte's *The Organization Man*, exploring the shift from inner-directed to other-directed personalities and the subjugation of the individual to their corporations. There can be little doubt, however, that his own individualism and non-participation in organizations on account of his parasitic anarchism, as well as the radical extremism of his thought, caused him to be marginalized not only academically but also intellectually. Although he has now written nine books, a mere four are listed in the Library of Congress catalogue and, while a work on the Victorian novelist Charles Reade was brought out commercially by Bookman Associates and another on Céline by Peter Lang, he has never been published by a mainstream firm let alone a university press. *Resisting Our Culture of Conformity* therefore deserves to be extensively read and Burns's ideas to become much better known. To assist in this process *Journey through the Dark Woods* and particularly *The Vanishing Individual* may be obtained at US$10 each plus postage from 212 East Howe Street, Seattle, WA 98102.

David Goodway

REVIEWS

Bakunin: The Creative Passion
Mark Leier
New York: St. Martins Press, 2006
ISBN 0-312-30538-9, $25-95

'Liberty without socialism is privilege and injustice; socialism without liberty is slavery and brutality' Bakunin (p190)

As I intimated in an earlier review (see *AS* 13 (1)), more than a decade ago I was prompted, indeed provoked, into writing a little introduction to the life and work of Michael Bakunin. My motivation for doing so was that I was not only incensed by the harsh, derogatory and unfair criticisms of Bakunin produced by liberal and Marxist scholars – who dismissed Bakunin as an intellectual buffoon bent on nothing but violence and destruction – but by anarcho-primitivists and Nietzschean individualists who completely repudiated Bakunin's social anarchism. For such fundamentalists Bakunin was a 'leftist' and not a real anarchist like themselves, and was thus best forgotten.

In his admirable study of Bakunin's philosophy, Paul McLoughlin has already done a great deal to restore Bakunin's intellectual integrity as a political thinker, underwriting his seminal importance in the development of social anarchism, as well as affirming that Bakunin is less of an historical curiosity than an anarchist whose ideas have a freshness and originality and a contemporary relevance which we would do well to examine and learn from. Complementing this work we now have Mark Leier's biography of Bakunin – subtitled 'The Creative Passion'. It is an excellent biography of the real Bakunin, not the caricature invoked by the likes of Aileen Kelly, Isaiah Berlin, Hal Draper and Francis Wheen – a biography long overdue.

Well researched and full of good scholarship Leier's biography is written in an engaging style, a style that is informative, insightful and full of zest, as Leier relates the many incidents and events in Bakunin's colourful and fascinating life. It is thus extremely readable, free of the kind of scholastic jargon that one usually encounters among so-called postmodern anarchists. In fact, Leier's biography is a delight to read, and at times quite entertaining, although occasionally his quips jar a little, especially if, like me, you have little interest in pop culture, comic strips and the Jerry Springer show.

What is helpful about Leier's biography is that not only does it offer an absorbing account of Bakunin's life, writings and political activities, but that it also provides a lot of useful background material regarding the sociohistorical context in which Bakunin lived and thought. There are, for example, extremely enlightening accounts of the following: Russian serfdom, the nature of capitalism as an economic system, the Paris

Commune, and German idealist philosophy – in which Leier delightfully summarizes the metaphysical ideas of Fichte and Hegel; as well as wonderful vignettes of Bakunin's contemporaries – Pierre-Joseph Proudhon, Wilhem Weitling and Sergei Nechaev. Interestingly though, Bakunin's more immediate comrades, Carlo Cafiero, Errico Malatesta, James Guillaume and Eliseé Reclus – all committed anarchist communists – get no more than a passing mention.

The main contours of Bakunin's turbulent life are perhaps well known, but Leier treats his subject with an unusual critical sympathy, giving a lucid and balanced account of the key issues and events surrounding Bakunin's life as a revolutionary anarchist. There are thus poignant discussions, by no means uncritical, of Bakunin's relationship with his immediate family, as well as his young wife Antonio; of Bakunin's penchant for secret societies; of the nature and context of his anti-Semitic outbursts; and of Bakunin's participation in the political insurrections in Dresden (1848) and Lyon (1870). Leier also gives a sympathetic and enlightening account of Bakunin's many years in prison (1849-1857) – two years of which were spent in solitary confinement in the infamous Peter and Paul Fortress. It was there that Bakunin penned his famous confession to the Tsar.

Throughout Leier's text there are also interesting insights into Bakunin's rather flamboyant personality; not for nothing did Richard Wagner and the Konigstein police describe him as a 'colossal'. By all accounts Bakunin had a warm, generous and outgoing personality, loved Beethoven's music, was seriously overweight, smoke and drank to excess, and unlike Marx was generally free of rancour, deceit and political intrigue. Leier affirms that Bakunin, given his generosity of spirit, had no ability as a political intriguer, despite his fondness for secret codes and imaginary organizations. He thus argues that there is absolutely no evidence at all that Bakunin ever wanted, or even tried, to take over or destroy the First International.

Besides providing us with a sensitive and poignant account of Bakunin's life and activities, as well as of the wider context, Leier's biography also gives succinct outlines of all Bakunin's major writings. These range from his early article 'The Reaction in Germany' (1842), which had a tremendous impact on his avant-garde contemporaries, to his last work 'Statism and Anarchy' (1873). The former article, on reactionary and reformist politics in Germany in the 1840s, ends with those famous words: 'The passion for destruction is at the same time a creative passion'. But as Leier makes clear this did not imply for Bakunin mindless violence or that he was prepared, like Attila and Robespierre, to 'wade though seas of blood' – as Isaiah Berlin churlishly put it – but rather it indicated the negation of the present social order (the overcoming of capitalism and the modern state) and the creation of a decentralized society based on voluntary associations. Moreover, as Leier emphasizes, this for Bakunin did not imply some apocalyptic vision – which is how Bakunin still continues to be understood, or rather misunderstood. Leier thus offers a clear riposte to those self-proclaimed post anarchists, like Richard Daly, who, putting new labels on old wine bottles, follow Bakunin's liberal and Marxist detractors, in seeing Bakunin as lost in some millennial or apocalyptic vision. And certainly, though Bakunin was an advocate of direct action and propaganda by the deed, and had sympathy for Russian brigands, he was never an advocate of assassinations, revolutionary violence or terrorism (unlike the youthful Engels). As Bakunin clearly put it: 'Liberty can only be created by liberty, by an insurrection of the people and the voluntary organization of the workers from below' (287). This entailed overcoming capitalism, and a complete break with all governments and bourgeois politics – a social revolution. As Leier writes: Bakunin 'insisted that revolutionary violence was to be directed against institutions not people, and nowhere did he advocate terrorism or assassination' (p208). In fact, Bakunin offered warnings against the harm caused by revolutionary violence, and had nothing but contempt for Nechaev's revolutionary nihilism and Jacobin politics. Bakunin's 'passion for destruction' did not then entail a cult of violence but a call to build gradually a new world free of oppression and exploitation. Bakunin's anarchism thus implied a philosophy of freedom, morality and solidarity; and the aim of a social revolution was not to kill individuals but to destroy 'property and the state' (p199).

Running through the book, almost like a silver thread, at least for the last two hundred pages, is a discussion of the complex relationship between Karl Marx and Bakunin. Leier, to his credit, tries not to take sides, and seems to act as a kind of broker, intent on bringing together Marxism (authoritarian socialism) and anarchism (libertarian socialism) – or 'collectivism' as Bakunin described his own brand of revolutionary or class struggle anarchism. Leier emphasizes that Marx and Bakunin had much in common besides their hirsute appearance; both came from privileged backgrounds and were radical democrats in their youth; both were philosophical realists and historical materialists; both were atheists, but sympathetic to the fact that religion often provided meaning, solace and consolation for the oppressed; both were committed members of the First International; both were essentially anti-capitalists – although Marx and Engels both sanctioned capitalist imperialism in relation to Morocco, India and the invasion of Mexico by the United States – Engels viewing such imperialism as in the interests of 'civilization'; and, finally, both remained dedicated revolutionary socialists to the end of their days. All this, despite the animosity that developed between the two men and their political differences. For Bakunin was always critical of Marx's authoritarian politics.

Director of the Centre for Labour Studies at Simon Fraser University, and author of several books on labour history, Mark Leier is to be complemented for providing us with a readable and very useful biography of Bakunin. Indeed, Leier specifically offers an interpretation of Bakunin's life and ideas that can be used by anyone interested in anarchism and social change. For Bakunin's critique of capitalism and the state has lost none of its force, and today, more than ever, Bakunin holds out a vision of a world of freedom, equality and fraternity against which the 'present reality' of global capitalism may be measured and found wanting. Such are the concluding words of this insightful biography. The book is indeed a timely affirmation of class struggle anarchism. It is a pity therefore that the book is only referenced with 'notes', and so there is no useable bibliography or even a listing of Bakunin's writings.

Brian Morris
Goldsmiths College

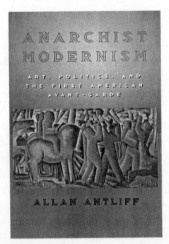